Copyright Notice

AWS Certified Solutions Architect Associate Exam

300+ Practice Questions

Disclaimer

This book was written as a study guide for obtaining AWS certification. While every effort has been made to make this book as accurate as possible no warranty is implied. The author shall not be liable or responsible for any loss or damage arising from the information contained in this book.

About The Author

Shaun Hummel is a Senior Network Engineer with 15+ years of network design, implementation and training experience across globally connected infrastructure. He is the author of multiple vendor certification books. The certification training strategy is based on a step-by-step approach with study guide and practice tests. It is all designed to prepare you for passing AWS associate certification.

Contents

Introduction

The skills required for I.T is changing rapidly with SDN, network programmability and automation. The virtualization of servers, applications and network devices is causing an overlap of management domains for network, systems and security engineers. The network devices and applications now reside at network servers as virtual machines (VM). In addition there is a shift toward an internet-based connectivity model that is changing how the network is managed. The server-centric architecture redefines how network capacity is managed as well. There are newer virtualized management solutions have been developed for integrating physical and virtual platforms.

Each group must develop new skills for virtualization, server-based troubleshooting and cloud management. The virtualization of applications and devices allow for an on-demand connectivity and operational model. It is characterized by a dynamic, elastic, scalable architecture that is hardware independent. The new networking paradigm uses Open APIs, overlays and SDN programmable network devices. The virtualization overlay abstracts the underlying network infrastructure from the application layer. The virtualization architecture is now enabling seamless access and global connectivity of enterprise and cloud data center applications.

The increasing popularity of cloud computing is the result of its operational model that now has enterprise companies migrating data center applications to cloud facilities. **According to a recent study almost 70% of all IP internet traffic is now terminating at a cloud facility**.

AWS certification has become popular as a training platform for systems administrators, engineers and architects. Candidates must answer technical questions and have the skills required to select, deploy, integrate and maintain AWS cloud solutions. The study guide is comprised of 300+ questions along with in-depth answers. All questions are based on official AWS certification guidelines that cover all exam topics required to pass *AWS Certified Solutions Architect Associate* exam. The question and answer format used in this book is an effective technique to learn and prepare for AWS certification.

Study Topics

Domain	Topics
EC2 Compute	AMI, EBS, Auto-Scaling, ElastiCache, ELB, ALB, EIP, Pricing Models, Instance Types, Resource Tags, SSH/RDP, Ping
Virtual Private Cloud	Routing Tables, Subnetting, Endpoints, Peering, DNS, DHCP, NAT Gateway, Security Groups, Network ACL, Internet Gateway, Virtual Private Gateway, Direct Connect, VPN IPsec
Storage Services	S3, Glacier, AWS Storage Gateway, Snowball, AWS Import/Export, EFS, Consistency Models
Security Architecture	Security Token Service (STS), Identity and Access Management (IAM), Shared Responsibility Model, Best Practices, KMS, Bastion Host, DDoS Mitigation, WAF, SSL/TLS, IDS/IPS, Host-Based Firewall, SAML, Web Identity Federation
Database Services	DynamoDB, RDS, MySQL, PostgreSQL, Redshift, EMR, Aurora
Fault Tolerant Systems	Route 53, RTO/RPO, Disaster Recovery Services, Snapshots, Multi-AZ
Deployment	API Gateway, SQS, Kinesis Streams, Firehose, Lambda, CORS, RESTful, JSON, CloudFront, Beanstalk, CloudFormation, OpsWorks, Data Pipeline, ECS, Stateless Systems, Loose Coupling
Monitoring Services	CloudWatch, CloudTrail, SNS, Flow Logs, Trusted Advisor

AWS Certified Solutions Architect - Associate Exam (SAA-C01)

The following is the official AWS Certified Solutions Architect Associate exam published guidelines.

Introduction

The AWS Certified Solutions Architect - Associate examination is intended for individuals who perform a Solutions Architect role. This exam validates an examinee's ability to effectively demonstrate knowledge of how to architect and deploy secure and robust applications on AWS technologies.

It validates an examinee's ability to:

- Define a solution using architectural design principles based on customer requirements.

- Provide implementation guidance based on best practices to the organization throughout the lifecycle of the project.

Recommended AWS Knowledge

- One year of hands-on experience designing fault-tolerant, cost-efficient, available and scalable distributed systems on AWS

- Hands-on experience using compute, networking, storage, and database AWS services

- Hands-on experience with AWS deployment and management services

- Ability to identify and define technical requirements for an AWS-based application

- Identify which AWS services meet a given technical requirement

- Knowledge of recommended best practices for building secure and reliable applications on the AWS platform

- An understanding of the basic architectural principles of building on the AWS cloud

- An understanding of the AWS global infrastructure

- An understanding of network technologies as they relate to AWS

- An understanding of security features and tools that AWS provides and how they relate to traditional services

Content Outline

1.0 Design Resilient Architectures

1.1 Choose reliable/resilient storage.

1.2 Determine how to design decoupling mechanisms using AWS services.

1.3 Determine how to design a multi-tier architecture solution.

1.4 Determine how to design high availability and/or fault tolerant architectures.

2.0 Define Performant Architectures

2.1 Choose performant storage and databases.

2.2 Apply caching to improve performance.

2.3 Design solutions for elasticity and scalability.

3.0 Specify Secure Applications and Architectures

3.1 Determine how to secure application tiers.

3.2 Determine how to secure data.

3.3 Define the networking infrastructure for a single VPC application.

4.0 Design Cost-Optimized Architectures

4.1 Determine how to design cost-optimized storage.

4.2 Determine how to design cost-optimized compute.

5.0 Define Operationally-Excellent Architectures

5.1 Choose design features in solutions that enable operational excellence.

EC2 Compute

Question 1:

What attributes are selectable when creating an EBS volume for an EC2 instance? (Select three)

A. volume type

B. IOPS

C. region

D. CMK

E. ELB

F. EIP

Answer

The tenant must select a volume type from general purpose (SSD), provisioned IOPS or HDD that enables performance and capacity. Volume type is selected based on application using the EBS volume and performance requirements. The default customer master key (CMK) encrypts an EBS store volume. The selected instance type assigned to any EC2 instance determines network capacity. AWS tenants can only assign an EBS volume to the same availability zone as the EC2 instance. (A,B,D)

Question 2:

You have been asked to migrate a 10 GB unencrypted EBS volume to an encrypted volume for security purposes. What are three key steps required as part of the migration?

A. pause the unencrypted instance

B. create a new encrypted volume of the same size and availability zone

C. create a new encrypted volume of the same size in any availability zone

D. start converter instance

E. shutdown and detach the unencrypted instance

Answer

The tenant first creates a new EBS encrypted volume of the same size as unencrypted volume. In addition the new encrypted volume is assigned to the same Availability Zone and encryption option is enabled. The convertor instance is started. The unencrypted EBS volume is shutdown and detached before starting data migration between volumes.

KMS is a key management service that generates customer master keys (CMK) used to create encrypted volumes and snapshots of encrypted volumes. There is a default CMK created by AWS for EBS volume encryption however tenants can create custom customer master keys. The encryption keys are then used to encrypt stored data at rest, in-transit and snapshots. Create an EBS snapshot of the unencrypted volume for backup before starting migration. (B,D,E)

Question 3:

What is EC2 instance protection?

A. prevents Auto Scaling from selecting specific EC2 instance to be replaced when scaling in

B. prevents Auto Scaling from selecting specific EC2 instance to be replaced when scaling out

C. prevents Auto Scaling from selecting specific EC2 instance for termination when scaling out

D. prevents Auto Scaling from selecting specific EC2 instance for termination when scaling in

E. prevents Auto Scaling from selecting specific EC2 instance for termination when paused

F. prevents Auto Scaling from selecting specific EC2 instance for termination when stopped

Answer

Capacity can be managed dynamically by adding instances (scaling out) or removing instances (scaling in) from an Auto-Scaling group. There is support for manually attaching and detaching instances, or automate capacity with a scaling policy. The termination policy is configured to select what instance is terminated first when automatic scaling in is enabled for an Auto-Scaling group. There is AWS instance protection available as well to prevent Auto Scaling from selecting specific instances for termination when scaling in. (D)

Question 4:

What two features are supported with EBS volume Snapshot feature?

A. EBS replication across regions

B. EBS multi-zone replication

C. EBS single region only

D. full snapshot data only

E. unencrypted snapshot only

Answer

EBS now supports replication of snapshots to multiple Availability Zones within a region and cross-region. The tenant must manually configure any cross-region replication from AWS services. There is a feature that copies over only snapshot changes making it faster and more cost effective. The tenant can snapshot encrypted and unencrypted EBS volumes. (A,B)

Figure 1 Copying an EBS Snapshot to a Different Availability Zone (Multi-AZ)

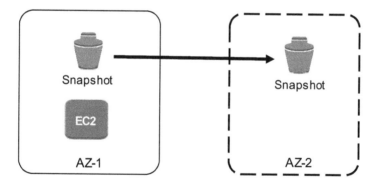

Question 5:

What two resource tags are supported for an EC2 instance?

A. VPC endpoint

B. EIP

C. network interface

D. security group

E. Flow Log

Answer

EC2 instance supports resource tags that are text strings with a key and optional value. The purpose is to categorize AWS resources by purpose, owner or environment. For example you could assign key = *testops*, value = *testsrv* to identify owner and project instance is assigned. (A,E)

Question 6:

What two options are available to alert tenants when an EC2 instance is terminated?

A. SNS

B. CloudTrail

C. Lambda function

D. SQS

E. STS

Answer

Amazon Simple Notification Service (SNS) can be configured to send a notification to a subscriber or endpoint when an EC2 instance is terminated from an Auto- Scaling group. The notification support includes HTTP, HTTPS, email or SQS message. In addition the tenant can create a Lambda function and route the termination event (trigger) to it. The Lambda function then logs the event to CloudWatch Logs. (A,C)

Question 7:

What class of EC2 instance type is recommended for running data analytics?

A. memory optimized

B. compute optimized

C. storage optimized

D. general purpose optimized

Answer

Compute optimized EC2 instances types are recommended for data analytics and processing intensive applications. There are subgroups of compute optimized instances as well designed for specific types of applications. (B)

Question 8:

What class of EC2 instance type is recommended for database servers?

A. memory optimized

B. compute optimized

C. storage optimized

D. general purpose optimized

Answer

Database servers are tables that contain large amounts of data for query and analysis. As a result they require memory optimized instances considering the fact that they increase over time as well. (A)

Question 9:

What two attributes distinguish each pricing model?

A. reliability

B. amazon service

C. discount

D. performance

E. redundancy

Answer

AWS pricing models are distinguished based on reliability and discounts. They provide capacity (compute + storage + network) and service levels for a variety of application requirements. (A,C)

Question 10:

What are three standard AWS pricing models?

A. elastic

B. spot

C. reserved

D. dynamic

E. demand

Answer

Demand model is based on a standard hourly usage, pay as you go, guaranteed access with no service interruption. It is recommended for short term bursty traffic requiring the same on-demand capacity as on-premises applications. Reserved mode provides up to 75% discounted pricing over demand model however not guaranteed to launch. It is based on availability and cloud traffic loads at that time. Assigning your instance to a specific Availability Zone provides some assurance of instance launch when required. It is recommended for applications where usage time and capacity are known.

Spot model provides up to 90% discount over demand model and based on any excess capacity that is available from Amazon when the instance is launched. The EC2 instances can be interrupted when required for on-demand usage tenant traffic. It is recommended for application profiles such as software development and testing, analytics, batch processing, fault tolerant failover activities and any processing that can be interrupted. (B,C,E)

Question 11:

How is an EBS root volume created when launching an EC2 instance from a new EBS-backed AMI?

A. S3 template

B. original AMI

C. snapshot

D. instance store

Answer

The root device storage is either instance store backed (S3) or an EBS-backed AMI used to launch an EC2 instance. The EBS root volume is equivalent to a hard drive for an EC2 instance or database instance. Tenants can attach additional EBS volumes that increase persistent storage available for the instance as well. The tenant can create a new AMI from an existing EC2 instance. Amazon EC2 creates a snapshot of your instance root volume and any other EBS volumes attached to your instance when creating a new AMI. During launch of an EC2 instance associated with the new AMI, there is a new EBS root volume created from the EBS snapshot. (C)

Figure 2 EC2 Instance Contents for EBS-backed Linux AMI

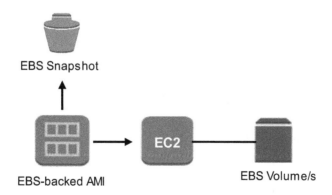

EBS Snapshot

EBS-backed AMI

EC2

EBS Volume/s

Question 12:

What Amazon AWS sources are available for creating an EBS-Backed Linux AMI? (select two)

A. EC2 instance

B. Amazon SMS

C. VM Import/Export

D. EBS Snapshot

E. S3 bucket

Answer

Tenants can create a new EBS-backed Linux AMI from an existing EC2 instance or an EBS Snapshot. The easiest method is to create a new AMI from an existing EBS-backed AMI. The tenant would launch an EC2 instance from the existing AMI and customize it for some new application. It is faster to start with a similar AMI than start from scratch. The EC2 instance is stopped and a new AMI is created and registered. (A,D)

Question 13:

What is required to prevent an instance from being launched and incurring costs?

A. stop instance

B. terminate instance

C. terminate AMI and de-register instance

D. stop and de-register instance

E. stop, deregister AMI and terminate instance

Answer

EC2 instances that are stopped or paused still incur some costs from AWS. You would stop your instance first before terminating to backup your data. That would include instance store to S3 or an EBS volume snapshot. The AMI is then deregistered to prevent launch and instance is terminated to stop billing. (E)

Question 14:

What is an EBS Snapshot?

A. backup of an EBS root volume and instance data

B. backup of an EC2 instance

C. backup of configuration settings

D. backup of instance store

Answer

EBS Snapshot is a backup of an EBS root volume and any additional EBS volumes (data) attached to an EC2 instance at a point in time. It is a bootable EBS volume that can launch EC2 instances and used to create additional AMI's when required. (A)

Question 15:

Where are ELB and Auto-Scaling groups deployed as a unified solution for horizontal scaling?

A. database instances

B. all instances

C. web server instances

D. default VPC only

Answer

It is the web server EC2 instances (front end tier) that support all of ELB and Auto-Scaling groups as a horizontal scaling solution. (C)

Question 16:

What feature is supported when attaching or detaching an EBS volume from an EC2 instance?

A. any available EBS volume can be attached and detached to an EC2 instance in the same region

B. any available EBS volume can be attached and detached to an EC2 instance that is cross-region

C. any available EBS volume can only be copied and attached to an EC2 instance that is cross-region

D. any available EBS volume can only be attached and detached to an EC2 instance in the same Availability Zone

Answer

Any available EBS volume can only be attached and detached to an EC2 instance in the same Availability Zone. The tenant must snapshot the volume, create a new volume and assign it to a different Availability Zone where the user or AWS service has IAM permissions. EBS volume can be attached to only one EC2 instance at a time. Multiple different EBS volumes can be attached to only one EC2 instance where one of the EBS volumes is the root device.

Amazon EBS provides General Purpose SSD (gp2), Provisioned IOPS SSD (io1), Throughput Optimized HDD (st1), Cold HDD (sc1) and Magnetic (older-generation type). Tenants can dynamically increase size, modify provisioned IOPS capacity and change volume type as well. (D)

Question 17:

What two statements correctly describe how to add or modify IAM roles to a running EC2 instance?

A. attach an IAM role to an existing EC2 instance from the EC2 console

B. replace an IAM role attached to an existing EC2 instance from the EC2 console

C. attach an IAM role to the user account and relaunch the EC2 instance

D. add the EC2 instance to a group where the role is a member

Answer

There is support now for attaching an IAM role to an existing EC2 instance from the EC2 console. You can also use the EC2 console to replace an IAM role attached to an existing instance. (A,B)

Question 18:

What is the default behavior for an EC2 instance when terminated? (Select two)

A. *DeleteOnTermination* attribute cannot be modified

B. EBS root device volume and additional attached volumes are deleted immediately

C. EBS data volumes that you attach at launch persist

D. EBS root device volume is automatically deleted when instance terminates

Answer

The EBS root device volume is automatically deleted when the instance is terminated. Any additional EBS volumes that were attached at launch persist (not deleted) in addition to EBS data volumes that you attach to an existing instance. The *DeleteOnTermination* attribute can be modified to False causing the EBS root volume to persist after termination. (C,D)

Question 19:

How do you launch an EC2 instance after it is terminated? (Select two)

A. launch a new instance using the same AMI

B. reboot instance from CLI

C. launch a new instance from a Snapshot

D. reboot instance from management console

E. contact AWS support to reset

Answer

It is not possible for a tenant to restart or connect to an EC2 instance after it has been terminated. The options are to launch a new instance using the same AMI associated with the instance or launch from an EBS snapshot previously made of the volume. (A,C)

Question 20:

What service can automate EBS snapshots (backups) for restoring EBS volumes?

A. CloudWatch event

B. SNS topic

C. CloudTrail

D. Amazon Inspector

E. CloudWatch alarm

Answer

CloudWatch events can be used to schedule automatic EBS snapshots at selected intervals. That is recommended for restoring an EBS volume with minimal data loss. The IAM events role is created and assigned from the console allowing CloudWatch to make EBS snapshot. (A)

Question 21:

What will cause AWS to terminate an EC2 instance on launch? (Select two)

A. security group error

B. number of EC2 instances on AWS account exceeded

C. EBS volume limits exceeded

D. multiple IP addresses assigned to instance

E. unsupported instance type assigned

Answer

There is an error message generated to the management console when an EC2 instance is terminated immediately on launch. Some of the typical causes include exceeded number of EC2 instances on AWS account and exceeded EBS volume limits. Specific limits that are exceeded will cause any new EC2 instances to terminate. (B,C)

Question 22:

You recently made some configuration changes to an EC2 instance. You launch a new EC2 instance from the same AMI however none of the settings are saved. What is the cause of this error?

A. did not save configuration changes to EC2 instance

B. did not save configuration changes to AMI

C. did not create new AMI

D. did not reboot EC2 instance to enable changes

Answer

Anytime you make configuration changes to an EC2 instance they only exist for that EC2 instance. Launching new EC2 instances from the same AMI will have the old configuration. The tenant must create a new AMI from the updated EC2 instance that can be used for launching additional instances with the desired settings. The changes could include a variety of settings including adding tags for instance. (C)

Question 23:

What two statements are correct concerning *DisableApiTermination* attribute?

A. cannot enable termination protection for Spot instances

B. termination protection is disabled by default for an EC2 instance

C. termination protection is enabled by default for an EC2 instance

D. can enable termination protection for Spot instances

E. *DisableApiTermination* attribute supported for EBS-backed instances only

Answer

Tenants can enable termination protection for an EC2 instance to prevent accidental termination from console, CLI or API. The termination protection is disabled by default. The *DisableApiTermination* attribute when changed to (true) enables termination protection. This feature is available for both Amazon EC2 instance store-backed (S3) and Amazon EBS-backed instances. There is no support for enabling termination protection on Spot instances. The Spot pricing model gives a two-minute warning before terminating an instance however. (A,B)

Question 24:

How is an encrypted EBS snapshot copied cross-account? (Select two)

A. copy the unencrypted EBS snapshot to an S3 bucket

B. distribute the custom key from CloudFront

C. share the custom key for the snapshot with the target account

D. share the encrypted EBS snapshot with the target account

E. share the encrypted EBS snapshots publicly

F. enable root access security on both accounts

Answer

Copying EBS encrypted snapshots between multiple AWS accounts and cross-region is now supported. It is common for tenants to create multiple AWS accounts based on function. That could include for example three accounts called development, testing and production. In addition data is moved between all three accounts based on the software lifecycle. As a result cross-account access is a key aspect of sharing data across the cloud.

The keys used to encrypt EBS snapshots (and other AWS data) is stored in and managed by AWS Key Management Service (KMS). The source account must create and share the custom key for the snapshot with the target account. In addition the encrypted EBS snapshot is shared with the target account. All of that is done from the IAM console where role or user permissions are granted. The target account user locates the EBS encrypted volume and select a different region from the source account. That is key when developers are located in different countries. There is no support for sharing EBS snapshots publicly. (C,D)

Question 25:

What AWS services enable Single-AZ only as a default? (Select three)

A. EC2

B. ELB

C. Auto-Scaling

D. DynamoDB

E. S3

Answer

EC2 instances, ELB and Auto-Scaling services are deployed to a single Availability Zone by default. AWS recommends you deploy them across multiple Availability Zones for redundancy and horizontal scaling. Amazon supports Multi-AZ for most services such as DynamoDB, RDS, S3 and SNS for example. AWS creates a default subnet in each Availability Zone (AZ) of the region where your VPC is located when **Default VPC** type is selected. EC2 instances however are not automatically replicated to each Availability Zone. (A,B,C)

Question 26:

What AWS service automatically publishes access logs every five minutes?

A. VPC Flow Logs

B. Elastic Load Balancer

C. CloudTrail

D. DNS Route 53

Answer

AWS require explicitly enabling logging and configuring IAM role permissions to publish the logs to CloudWatch Log group. The CloudWatch service is called CloudWatch Logs where they are centralized. Elastic Load Balancer when enabled, publishes data to an access log at 5-minute intervals. That includes each request to the load balancer with source IP address and server response. Log files for AWS services are stored in an S3 bucket and where enabled published to CloudWatch Logs. The tenant must grant each AWS services write (PutObject) permission to the S3 bucket. (B)

Question 27:

You have developed a web-based application for file sharing that will allow customers to access files. There are a variety of sizes that include larger .pdf and video files. What two solution stacks could tenants use for an online file sharing service? (Select two)

A. EC2, ELB, Auto-Scaling, S3

B. Route 53, Auto-Scaling, DynamoDB

C. EC2, Auto-Scaling, RDS

D. CloudFront

Answer

Minimum requirements are EC2 instances for front end web servers, ELB to distribute requests across multiple servers, Auto-Scaling for fault tolerance and S3 storage. The tenant would enable Multi-AZ for redundancy, basic security access and CloudWatch monitoring as well. There is CloudFront as an alternative that is preferred for multi-region (global) customers. (A,D)

Question 28:

What infrastructure services are provided to EC2 instances? (Select three)

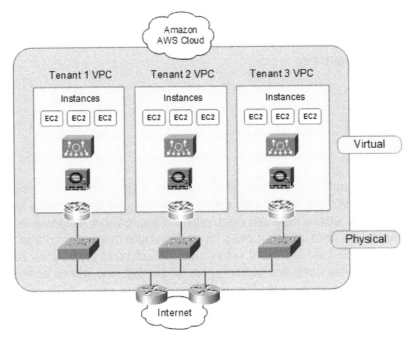

A. VPN

B. storage

C. compute

D. transport

E. security

F. support

Answer

Some of the IaaS services provided by Amazon AWS include compute, data storage and network transport within the data center. Any external WAN connectivity is provided by customers (tenants) to the enterprise. (B,C,D)

Question 29:

What steps are required from AWS console to copy an EBS-backed AMI for a database instance cross-region?

A. create Snapshot of data volume, select Copy, select destination region

B. select Copy EBS-backed AMI option and destination region

C. select copy database volume and destination region

D. create Snapshot of EBS-backed AMI, select Copy Snapshot option, select destination region

E. create Snapshot of Instance-store AMI, select Copy AMI option, select destination region

Answer

Anytime you make a copy of an AMI it is the instance configuration only and does not include any session data. The Snapshot includes the EBS root volume (for boot) and all EBS data volumes for the instance. That creates an instance that can boot (launch) and have all data volumes attached. The tenant would take a Snapshot of the EBS- backed AMI and select *Copy SnapShot* option where destination region is specified. Launching the database instance from that AMI would include all session data up to the point on time when Snapshot was taken.

The same is true for a Snapshot of an AMI comprised of a web server EC2 instance. This illustrates a key aspect of an AMI vs an AMI backed by EBS volume Snapshot. The instance type determines whether the AMI is instance store-backed (S3) or EBS backed volume. You can select to encrypt the Snapshot with the default CMK or specify a custom key. (D)

Question 30:

How is capacity (compute, storage and network speed) managed and assigned to EC2 instances?

A. AMI

B. instance type

C. IOPS

D. Auto-Scaling

Answer

The tenant selects and assigns an Amazon EC2 instance type to an instance based on requirements. The capacity planning paradigm shifts somewhat now that the underlying throughput is based on server hardware. Traditional network capacity is based on physical network devices. Cloud virtual appliances and servers are converted to EC2 instances (virtual machines). The cloud provider defines multiple instance types that customers can assign to each server or virtual appliance. Some virtual appliances only support specific EC2 instance types and maximum throughput licensing.

By contrast, the capacity of unlicensed appliances are limited by network design and the EC2 instance type assigned. The EC2 instance type selected directly affect network design and performance. Throughput can be increased for some virtual appliances with license upgrades. The EC2 instance type is based on capacity requirements and network design. Selecting the correct instance type is a key aspect of capacity planning and cloud performance. N-tier applications are comprised of multiple servers with varying requirements. Discuss the cloud migration with the application vendor for optimal recommendations. (B)

Question 31:

What storage type enable permanent attachment of volumes to EC2 instances?

A. S3

B. RDS

C. TDS

D. EBS

E. instance store

Answer

EBS architecture allows the tenant to attach permanent storage volumes to server EC2 instances. The EBS volume size is configured at the time an instance is defined. EC2 instance store is similar to RAM where session data is deleted when the instance is stopped, terminated or problems occur. The session data is not deleted however when the instance is rebooted. (D)

Question 32:

What is the recommended method for migrating (copying) an EC2 instance to a different region?

A. terminate instance, select region, copy instance to destination region

B. select AMI associated with EC2 instance and use *Copy AMI* option

C. stop instance and copy AMI to destination region

D. cross-region copy is not currently supported

Answer

Amazon AWS does not permit copy of an EC2 instance within or cross-region. It does however allow copying the AMI associated with the EC2 instance. The tenant would select the AMI and then Copy AMI option where destination region is specified. That would make the AMI available in the destination region to launch the EC2 instance. Any launch permissions, user-defined tags or S3 bucket permissions are not copied from the source AMI to the new AMI. (B)

Question 33:

What are two attributes that define an EC2 instance type?

A. vCPU

B. license type

C. EBS volume storage

D. IP address

E. Auto-Scaling

Answer

The hardware capacity and features vary for each instance type. The standard features include number of vCPU cores, memory, disk space, throughput and network interfaces. Instance types are either based on instance storage or EBS volume storage. In addition there are storage optimized instance types for attached EBS volumes. That allows for increased IOPS and interface throughput. Amazon has an enhanced networking feature as well that are available with some instance types. It provides increased throughput in addition to lower latency and jitter. (A,C)

Question 34:

How is an Amazon Elastic Load Balancer (ELB) assigned?

A. per EC2 instance

B. per Auto-Scaling group

C. per subnet

D. per VPC

Answer

EC2 elastic architecture is an Amazon AWS feature that optimizes availability and provides on-demand capacity to tenants. The tenant can register one or multiple EC2 instances to an Elastic Load Balancer (ELB). Auto-Scaling aggregates multiple EC2 instances (servers) to group for horizontal scaling purposes. ELB distributes ingress cloud traffic among available EC2 instances within a single or multiple Auto-Scaling groups. It will monitor server health and failover user sessions to available servers. That would include load balancing servers across Availability Zones at redundant data centers. (A)

Question 35:

What method is used for detecting when to replace an EC2 instance that is assigned to an Auto-Scaling group?

A. health check

B. load balancing algorithm

C. EC2 health check

D. dynamic path detection

Answer

Elastic Load Balancers runs health checks to detect when web server EC2 instances are unavailable or over-utilized. It is the Auto-Scaling group that is notified and replaces the EC2 instance. The advantage of ELB health check is that it provides application level status. (A)

The EC2 status check (default) is hypervisor level and verifies up/down status only. Tenants can offload SSL processing from web servers to Elastic Load Balancers as well. That enables SSL acceleration for web-based applications using SSL encryption with browsers. The following describe the steps for configuring an Elastic Load Balancer:

1. Select ELB service from Amazon AWS management console
2. Create the load balancer and assign a name
3. Enable HTTPS protocol as listener for tenant sessions
4. Configure custom health checks for server utilization and network latency
5. Assign the web server EC2 instances
6. Add VeriSign SSL certificate and keys for SSL acceleration

Question 36:

What two statements correctly describe Auto-Scaling groups?

A. horizontal scaling of capacity

B. decrease number of instances only

C. EC2 instances are assigned to a group

D. database instances only

E. no support for multiple availability zones

Answer

Cloud provider model allow tenants to offload bursty workloads and traffic peaks to maintain performance. Any unused CPU processing is allocated somewhere else when there is no traffic. The traffic for most applications will often increase over time. The Auto Scaling feature allows the tenant to seamlessly increase aggregate server capacity based on throughput requirements. It is a horizontal scaling of capacity to a server group based on performance thresholds. The number of EC2 instances assigned to an Auto Scaling group increase or decrease based on any exceeded thresholds. It is a service designed specifically for front-end EC2 instances and not database instances. (A,C)

Question 37:

What is the default maximum number of Elastic IP addresses assignable per Amazon AWS region?

A. 1

B. 100

C. 5

D. unlimited

Answer

AWS Elastic Network Interfaces (ENI) are virtual network interfaces assigned to an EC2 instances (including virtual appliances) within a VPC. The ENI supports multiple private IP addresses assignable per interface. The tenant can assign a single Elastic IP (public) or public IPv4 address as well to the same interface. The tenant is assigned five static public Elastic IP (EIP) addresses per region.

There are often multiple public web servers deployed across availability zones. The solution, where additional are required, is to use NAT or request some additional EIP addresses from Amazon. The addresses 10.0.0.1 – 10.0.0.4 is reserved by Amazon AWS for each subnet range. In addition ENI supports multiple IPv6 addresses, security groups, MAC address and source/destination check attribute. (C)

Question 38:

How are snapshots for an EBS volume created when it is the root device for an instance?

A. pause instance, unmount volume and snapshot

B. terminate instance and snapshot

C. unencrypt volume and snapshot dynamically

D. stop instance, unmount volume and snapshot

Answer

The recommended procedure is to stop the EC2 instance, unmount the volume and Snapshot the EBS volume for best results. (D)

Question 39:

What cloud compute (EC2 instances) components are configured by tenants and not Amazon AWS support engineers? (Select three)

A. hypervisor

B. upstream physical switch

C. virtual appliances

D. guest operating system

E. applications and databases

F. RDS

Answer

The tenant is responsible for configuring the guest operating system and all application level settings including database structures and associated security access. That would include any security groups and ACLs assigned to a VPC. In addition any virtual appliances deployed to the VPC are configured by tenants based on their requirements. The configuration settings become part of the AMI bundle created for each EC2 instance. Amazon AWS creates the instances and configures the operating system for managed services such as RDS. (C,D,E)

Question 40:

What three attributes are used to define a launch configuration template for an Auto-Scaling group?

A. instance type

B. network ACL

C. private IP address

D. Elastic IP

E. security group

F. AMI

Answer

Auto-Scaling groups are defined with an initial number of EC2 instances that enable horizontal scaling. The scaling policy is used to increase or decrease the number of EC2 instances for a group based on utilization (workload). The launch template creates an automatic launch configuration that supports multiple versions with different launch configurations. The configuration attributes include AMI ID, instance type, key pair, security group/s and block device mapping.

EC2 instances for the same server group (i.e web servers) are launched from a single AMI. Private IP addressing is automatically assigned to instances from a DHCP server. The tenant cannot explicitly assign EIP or network ACL from a launch configuration. The options for creating an Auto-Scaling group include launch template, launch configuration or EC2 instance (manual). (A,E,F)

Question 41:

What three characteristics or limitations differentiate EC2 instance types?

A. VPC only

B. application type

C. EBS volume only

D. virtualization type

E. AWS service selected

Answer

EC2 instance types are selected based on the application being deployed and specific capacity requirements. The characteristics of an EC2 instance include compute, storage, memory and networking features. In addition there are limitations such as VPC only launch, EBS only volumes and virtualization type. Most of the current generation instance types require HVM. (A,C,D)

Question 42:

What are the two difference between HVM and PV virtualization types?

A. HVM supports all current generation instance types

B. HVM is similar to bare metal hypervisor architecture

C. PV provides better performance than HVM for most instance types

D. HVM does not support enhanced networking

E. HVM does not support current generation instance types

Answer

Current generation instance types all support HVM virtualization type however only C3 and M3 support PV virtualization types as well. The advantages of HVM include enhanced networking support with hardware extensions and hardware virtualization. The hardware extensions provide optimize performance for instances. The hardware virtualization (isolation) enables migration of EC2 instances across various hardware platforms. That permits instances to run operating systems on different hardware platforms without modifications. (A,B)

Virtual Private Cloud (VPC)

Question 1:

What are the minimum components required to enable a web-based application with public web servers and a private database tier? (Select three)

A. Internet gateway

B. Assign EIP addressing to database instances on private subnet

C. Virtual private gateway

D. Assign database instances to private subnet and private IP addressing

E. Assign EIP and private IP addressing to web servers on public subnet

Answer

Each EC2 instance is assigned at least a single private IP address for VPC routing. The web servers are assigned to a public subnet. In addition each server is assigned a private IP address and a public EIP address. The EIP is used to advertise IP addressing across the internet. The tenant will attach a single Amazon Internet gateway to the VPC for public internet access. The database servers are assigned to a private subnet and private IP addressing only. There are no incoming sessions allowed from the internet to the private subnets. The tenant can assign a NAT instance to a public subnet. That will forward traffic from private subnets to public subnet and Internet gateway for direct internet access.

The servers assigned to private subnets can then connect to internet-based S3 storage as well. Any public EC2 instance without a public EIP address can use the NAT assigned EIP for internet access as well. The tenant would typically subnet the VPC CIDR block of 10.0.0.0/16 to a smaller 10.0.0.0/24 CIDR block. The /24 subnet mask provides 256 private IP addresses per subnet. (A,D,E)

Question 2:

Refer to the network drawing. How are packets routed from private subnet to public subnet for the following web-based application with a database tier?

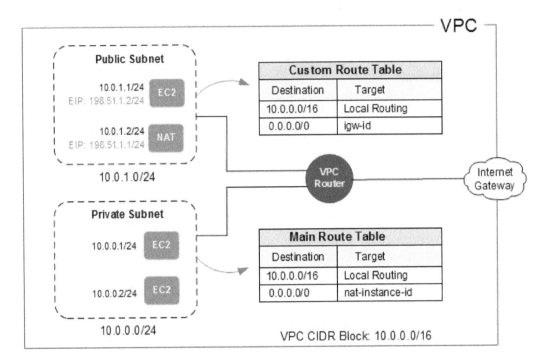

A. Internet gateway

B. custom route table

C. 10.0.0.0/16

D. nat-instance-id

E. igw-id

F. add custom route table

Answer

The network drawing is a web-based application with a web server in the public subnet and database tier in the private subnet. NAT instance is required in the public subnet. The *nat-instance-id* with 0.0.0.0/0 route in the main route table is used to forward packets from the private subnet to web server in the public subnet. (D)

Question 3:

What VPC component provides Network Address Translation?

A. NAT instance

B. NAT gateway

C. Virtual private gateway

D. Internet gateway

E. ECS

Answer

Internet gateway provides access to the internet for all EC2 instances within a VPC. In addition it provides 1:1 network address translation from private addressing to public addressing for the VPC. There is horizontal scaling with virtually no bandwidth limits. The network capacity limits occur with EC2 instances or internet connection speed. (D)

Question 4:

What are the advantages of NAT gateway over NAT instance? (Select two)

A. NAT gateway requires a single EC2 instance

B. NAT gateway is scalable

C. NAT gateway translates faster

D. NAT gateways is a managed service

E. NAT gateway is Linux-based

Answer

The NAT gateway or NAT instance enables an EC2 instance to initiate outbound packets from a private subnet to a public subnet. VPC does not allow traffic to flow directly from private to public subnets for security reasons without that. It is not the same as traditional network address translation. There is an EIP assigned to the NAT service that enables packet forwarding packets to the public subnet. The NAT gateway is a managed service that does not require the tenant to have a running EC2 instance. It is more scalable than NAT instance with 10 Gbps throughput for faster applications and redundant. There is no support for associating security groups with the NAT gateway. (B,D)

Question 5:

What is the management responsibility of tenants and not Amazon AWS?

A. EC2 instances

B. RDS

C. Beanstalk

D. NAT instance

Answer

EC2 instances including NAT instance are managed by the tenant. Software maintenance, security updates, managing instance failures and security group rules are the responsibility of tenants. Managing the underlying hosts for RDS and Beanstalk is the responsibility of AWS. (A,D)

Question 6:

What two features provide an encrypted (VPN) connection from VPC to an enterprise data center?

A. Internet gateway

B. Amazon RDS

C. Virtual private gateway

D. CSR 1000V router

E. NAT gateway

Answer

The two primary options for connecting the enterprise data center to a VPC are the Virtual Private Gateway (VPG) and Cisco CSR 1000V router. In addition there is CloudHub that is designed for easier connectivity of multiple branch offices. There is support for static routing or BGP dynamic routing with assigned ASN 64512. All data is encrypted with IPsec using AES256 cipher. (C,D)

Figure 3 Public and VPN Subnet Model

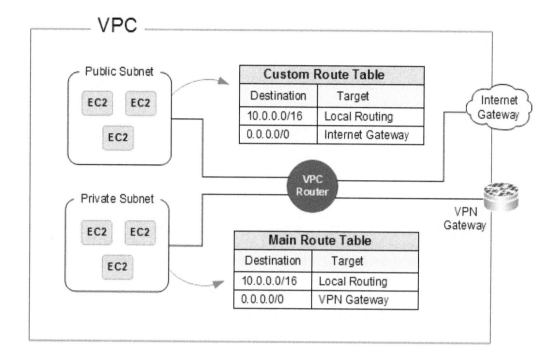

Question 7:

What two attributes are supported when configuring an Amazon Virtual private gateway (VPG)?

A. route propagation

B. Elastic IP (EIP)

C. DHCP

D. public IPv4 address

E. public subnets

Answer

Route propagation automatically installs local routes in the main route table for advertising to a peering customer gateway. There is a default route as well in the main route table (vgw-id 0.0.0.0/0). Local EC2 instances use that route for access to the Virtual private gateway connection. The tenant can forward requests to a private on-premises DHCP server as well for VPN connections. (A,C)

Question 8:

What two features are available with AWS Direct Connect service?

A. internet access

B. extend on-premises VLANs to cloud

C. bidirectional forwarding detection (BFD)

D. load balancing between Direct Connect and VPN connection

E. public and private AWS services

Answer

Direct Connect provides access at the AWS cloud connection point to all AWS public and private services through virtual interfaces. The public virtual interfaces are configured at the tenant colocated router for accessing S3 and Glacier storage services. In addition private virtual interfaces are configured for VPC access where application EC2 instances reside. The purpose of BFD is to detect link failure and do fast failover to a standby link such as VPN IPsec.

Direct Connect is a private and not internet-based service that is not a solution for extending on-premises VLANs to the AWS cloud. There is no active/active topology available either negating any load balancing to the cloud. (C,E)

Figure 4 Direct Connect Architecture

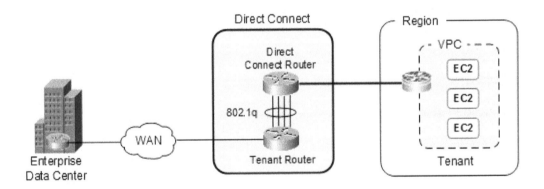

Question 9:

When is Direct Connect a preferred solution over VPN IPsec?

A. fast and reliable connection

B. redundancy is a key requirement

C. fast and easy to deploy

D. layer 3 connectivity

E. layer 2 connectivity

Answer

The purpose of AWS Direct Connect is to enabled a private dedicated connection between on-premises and AWS cloud. It is often used for backups, real-time replication for hybrid cloud solutions. There is a top speed of 10 Gbps that is reliable and unaffected by any internet latency and congestions. The high performance can result in costs that are competitive or lower than internet. There is no redundancy or load balancing across multiple connections. Failover options are a second Direct Connect service or VPN IPsec connection. (A)

Question 10:

You have been asked to setup a VPC endpoint connection between VPC and S3 buckets for storing backups and snapshots. What AWS components are currently required when configuring a VPC endpoint?

A. Internet gateway

B. NAT instance

C. Elastic IP

D. private IP address

E. Direct Connect

Answer

VPC endpoints enable tenants to create a connection from VPC to S3 with private IP addressing only. All routing as a result is directly from a private subnet with the main route table. There is no requirement or support for the traditional solution of an Internet gateway or NAT instance. Traffic is internal to the Amazon AWS cloud eliminating any support for cross-region requests.

By extension any external links such as VPN IPsec and Direct connect are not supported for VPC endpoints. There is no VPC peering permitted considering traffic does not leave the source VPC. AWS permits security policies that are endpoint centric for managing access to S3 buckets as an additional layer of security where there are existing bucket permissions. VPC endpoint default policy is to allow full access to S3 buckets where there is no bucket-level or object-level permissions. (D)

Figure 5 VPC Endpoint for Private Connectivity to S3 Storage

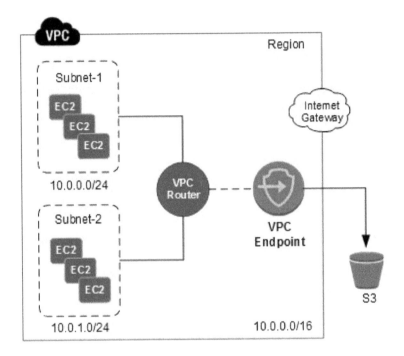

Question 11:

What are the primary advantages of VPC endpoints? (Select two)

A. reliability

B. cost

C. throughput

D. security

Answer

The primary reason for deploying VPC endpoints is to minimize the costs associated with internet connectivity for S3, DynamoDB and Kinesis traffic classes. It is preferable as well to avoid performance problems inherent with internet connections. In addition all traffic remains within the AWS cloud and does not traverse the internet. That is preferred for applications with security compliance requirements. (B,D)

Question 12:

What are the DHCP option attributes used to assign tenant-managed private DNS servers to your VPC?

A. dns resolution
   domain name

B. hostnames
   internet domain

C. domain servers
   domain name

D. domain-name-servers
   domain-name

Answer

The tenant must change both DNS attributes to false (no) and modify DHCP options that point to private DNS servers managed by the tenant and customized DNS hostnames. The DHCP attributes "domain-name-servers" allow four private DNS servers to be specified. In addition the "domain-name" attribute is configured for the company domain name assigned. (D)

- DNS resolution: no (disable AWS DNS and use tenant private DNS servers)
- DNS hostnames: no (tenant custom public and/or private DNS hostnames)

Question 13:

What DNS attributes are configured when **Default VPC** option is selected?

A. DNS resolution: yes
   DNS hostnames: yes

B. DNS resolution: yes
   DNS hostnames: no

C. DNS resolution: no
   DNS hostnames: yes

D. DNS resolution: no
   DNS hostnames: no

Answer

When an EC2 instance is launched into a default VPC, AWS provides the instance with public and/or private DNS hostnames that correspond to the public IPv4 and private IPv4 addresses for the EC2 instance.

- DNS resolution: **yes** (enable AWS provided DNS services)
- DNS hostnames: **yes** (AWS assigns private and/or public DNS hostnames)

When an instance is launched into a **Nondefault VPC**, Amazon AWS provides each instance with a private DNS hostname. In addition a public DNS hostname is provided only when DNS hostnames attribute is changed from no to yes and your instance is using a public IPv4 address. (A)

Question 14:

What configuration settings are required from the remote VPC in order to create cross-account peering? (Select three)

A. VPC ID

B. account username

C. account ID

D. CMK keys

E. VPC CIDR block

F. volume type

Answer

Amazon AWS does support VPC peering between two different AWS accounts. The required information includes neighbor VPC ID, account ID and VPC CIDR block. The VPC ID and account ID are administrative attributes that identify the AWS customer account. The tenant must add a route to the local main route table as well that points to the neighbor CIDR block range. The IAM cross-account access role is assigned to the initiating tenant from the neighbor that allows connection setup. (A,C,E)

Question 15:

What CIDR block range is supported for IPv4 addressing and subnetting within a single VPC?

A. /16 to /32

B. /16 to /24

C. /16 to /28

D. /16 to /20

Answer

The CIDR block range supported for IPv4 addressing and subnetting within a single VPC is /16 to /28. That would for instance include 10.0.0.0/16 to 10.0.0.0/28 CIDR block range for that private subnet addressing selected. Note that /32 is used to configure a host address and is not a subnet. (C)

Question 16:

What problem is caused by the fact that VPC peering does not permit transitive routing?

A. additional VPC route tables to manage

B. Virtual private gateway is required

C. Internet gateway is required for each VPC

D. routing between connected spokes through hub VPC is complex

E. increased number of peer links required

Answer

There is no support for transitive routing between VPC peering links. VPC peering is based on private cloud-only links that are point-to-point between each VPC. Tenants cannot use a hub VPC for routing packets between two connected spoke VPCs. The spoke VPCs must be directly connected to exchange routes. The result is additional VPC links and routing between them. (E)

Question 17:

What two statements correctly describes Elastic Load Balancer operation?

A. spans multiple regions

B. assigned per EC2 instance

C. assigned per subnet

D. assigned per Auto-Scaling group

E. no cross-region support

Answer

One or multiple Elastic Load Balancers (ELB) are attached to an existing Auto Scaling group. ELB automatically registers the instances and distributes incoming traffic across the instances. The ELB enters the *Adding* state while registering the instances in the group and then it enters the *Added* state. The ELB enters *InService* state after at least one registered instance passes the health checks . Auto-Scaling does not terminate and replace EC2 instances unless ELB enters *InService* state. Note that EC2 instances remain running after they are deregistered from an ELB. There is cross-region support for load balancing available with DNS Route 53 service. (D,E)

Figure 6 Elastic Load Balancers and Cross-Zone Auto-Scaling Groups

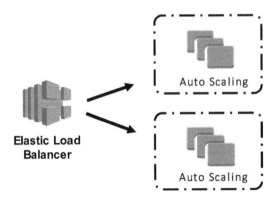

Question 18:

What are two advantages of Elastic IP (EIP) over AWS public IPv4 addresses?

A. EIP can be reassigned

B. EIP is private

C. EIP is dynamic

D. EIP is persistent

E. EIP is public and private

Answer

Public IPv4 addresses are not reassignable or persistent. Amazon AWS returns public IPv4 addresses to a shared pool for multi-tenant usage. EIP is a static internet routable IP address that can be manually reassigned to another instance when there is an instance failure. Dynamic IP address assignments are based on DHCP. Amazon automatically assigns a public IPv4 address to an instance network interface when the tenant disassociates an EIP from it. The public internet is accessed through the VPC Internet gateway. (A,D)

Question 19:

What AWS services are globally managed? (Select four)

A. IAM

B. S3

C. CloudFront

D. Route 53

E. DynamoDB

F. WAF

G. ELB

Answer

Most AWS services are regional-based where they reside in a single or multiple Availability Zones. There is support as well for deploying the same services cross- region. The services that are globally managed include IAM, Route 53, CloudFront and WAF. The tenant does not have to recreate or copy anything between regions to enable features or change configuration. IAM is a unified security schema that is not assigned to any particular region.

Security groups and ACLs are assigned to a VPC and are not global. In addition resource policies such as permissions assigned to a bucket are not global either. Route 53 is a global load balancer that forwards packets to an Elastic Load Balancers in Availability Zones. CloudFront is deployed globally to multiple edge locations globally along with WAF for malware packet inspection. (A,C,D,F)

Question 20:

What standard methods are available for creating a VPC? (Select three)

A. AWS management console

B. AWS marketplace

C. VPC wizard

D. VPC console

E. Direct Connect

Answer

The VPC wizard is designed to automatically deploy a VPC based on your design requirements. The tenant would select one of four standard designs that deploy a subnetting model:

- public subnet only
- public subnet and private subnet
- public subnet and VPN-only subnet
- VPN-only subnet

In addition there is VPC console where the tenant can select either a default VPC or nondefault VPC. Amazon AWS will then programmatically configure and deploy the VPC based on what was selected. The nondefault VPC as the name suggests permits the tenant to configure nondefault subnet addressing and does not add any gateway. It is now possible as well for tenants to create a default VPC from the AWS management console or CLI. (A,C,D)

Question 21:

What two default settings are configured for tenants by AWS when **Default VPC** option is selected?

A. creates a size /20 default subnet in each Availability Zone

B. creates an Internet gateway

C. creates a main route table with local route 10.0.0.0/16

D. create a virtual private gateway

E. create a security group that explicitly denies all traffic

Answer

Amazon AWS creates a default VPC CIDR block (172.31.0.0/16) that is subnetted with default subnets from 172.31.0.0/20 addressing. There is a default subnet created in each Availability Zone for the AWS region where the VPC is located. Your Default VPC is connected to an Internet gateway and EC2 instances automatically receive public IPv4 addresses.

The main route table has 172.31.0.0/16 as a local route added as well. There is a default security group that permits all traffic inbound and outbound. By default Amazon selects an Availability Zone and launches the EC2 instance into the subnet associated with that Availability Zone. That only occurs when the tenant launches an EC2 instance without specifying a subnet. (A,B)

Question 22:

What three statements correctly describes IP address allocation within a VPC?

A. EC2 instance must be terminated to reassign an IP address

B. EC2 instance that is paused can reassign IP address

C. EC2 instance that is stopped can reassign IP address

D. private IP addresses are allocated from a pool and can be reassigned

E. private IP addresses can be assigned by tenant

F. VPC supports dual stack mode (IPv4/IPv6)

Answer

Elastic IP addresses are statically assigned to an AWS tenant account while public IPv4 addresses are allocated from a pool. it is possible to reassign an EIP however public IPv4 addresses are released to a common pool when not used and randomly selected. The primary private IP address assigned to each instance cannot be reassigned as well.

When launching an instance into a VPC, you can optionally assign a primary private IP address from the IPv4 address range of the subnet or AWS will assign it from the subnet range. The private address is assigned to the default network interface (eth0) of the instance. You can add multiple secondary private IP addresses that are often used for virtual appliances. EC2 instances must be terminated to reassign an Elastic IP address to a new EC2 instance. (A,E,F)

Question 23:

What are two advantages of selecting default tenancy option for your VPC when creating it?

A. performance and reliability

B. some AWS services do not work with a dedicated tenancy VPC

C. tenant can launch instances within VPC as default or dedicated instances

D. instance launch is faster

E. dedicated and host tenancy require expensive instance types

Answer

The advantages of selecting default tenancy for your VPC is compatibility with AWS services and launch support. Default tenancy permits tenants to launch an EC2 instance as a default (shared hardware) or dedicated (single-tenant) isolated hardware. Creating a VPC with dedicated tenancy only allows EC2 instances to launch as dedicated or host.

You cannot run instances with default (shared) tenancy. There is dedicated host option as well that assigns a physical server to a tenant for running instances. The host option is typically required for licensing or security compliance requirements. The advantages of dedicated and host tenancy is performance, reliability and security. Some AWS services do not work with a dedicated tenancy VPC and there is increased cost. The choice is based on requirements for performance and security. (B,C)

Question 24:

What is the purpose of a local route within a VPC route table?

A. local route is derived from the default VPC CIDR block 10.0.0.0/16

B. communicate between instances within the same subnet or different subnets

C. used to communicate between instances within the same subnet

D. default route for communicating between private and public subnets

E. only installed in the main route table

Answer

The local route is used for communicating between instances within the same subnet only. Any communication between subnets requires the native VPC router. Forwarding packets between private and public subnets requires NAT.

The local route is the top level CIDR subnet used to create VPC subnets. It varies based on whether it is a default VPC (default subnet 172.31.0.0/16), VPC created by the VPC wizard (10.0.0.0/16) or tenant custom addressing. There is a local route installed in the main route table and each custom route table. (C)

Question 25:

What is the default behavior when adding a new subnet to a VPC? (Select two)

A. new subnet is associated with the main route table

B. new subnet is associated with the custom route table

C. new subnet is associated with any selected route table

D. new subnet is assigned to the default subnet

E. new subnet is assigned from the VPC CIDR block

Answer

Any new subnet is associated with the main route table by default. The tenant can then reassign the subnet to a custom route table based on routing requirements. The main route table cannot be deleted and can be assigned to private or public subnets.

It is typically used for private subnets however the tenant could for example deploy a single subnet with some public web servers (with EIP's) to a main route table and advertise to the internet. The main route table has a default route (0.0.0.0/0) to the Internet gateway if it is created with default VPC option. (A,E)

Question 26:

You have enabled Amazon RDS database services in VPC1 for an application that has public web servers in VPC2. How do you connect the web servers to the RDS database instance so they can communicate considering the VPC's are in the same region?

A. VPC endpoints

B. VPN gateway

C. path-based routing

D. VPC peering

E. AWS Network Load Balancer

Answer

The web server EC2 instances can communicate with an RDS database instance across a VPC peering link. VPC peering connection is a direct private connection between two VPCs that enables you to route traffic between them using private IP addresses. Instances in either VPC can communicate with each other and traffic remains within Amazon AWS cloud (not internet). The VPC peering feature can link different AWS accounts as well. (D)

Question 27:

What AWS services now support VPC endpoints feature for optimizing security? (Select three)

A. Kinesis

B. DNS Route 53

C. S3

D. DynamoDB

E. RDS

Answer

VPC endpoints enable EC2 instances in private subnets to communicate directly with supported AWS services from within AWS cloud instead of traversing the internet. Previously all S3, DynamoDB and Kinesis traffic required an Internet gateway. The primary advantage is security where all traffic between EC2 instances and AWS services mentioned remain within the AWS cloud.

In addition usage costs for Internet gateway and NAT are eliminated for that traffic class. VPN connections and Direct Connect can be eliminated for some deployments as well. The VPC endpoint is an Elastic Network Interface (ENI) with a private IP address assigned or AWS Private Link service. The ENI is nothing more than the EC2 instance interface that supports multiple public and/or private IP addresses. There is a Network Load Balancer that forwards requests to AWS services from a VPC endpoint for network level connectivity. (A,C,D)

Question 28:

What are three characteristics of an Amazon Virtual Private Cloud?

A. public and private IP addressing

B. broadcasts

C. multiple private IP addresses per network interface

D. dedicated single tenant hardware only

E. persistent public IP addresses

F. HSRP

Answer

Amazon VPC architecture allows for virtual appliances that enable network services similar to the enterprise data center. The VPC supports assigning multiple private IP addresses to network interfaces on virtual appliances called virtual service nodes. There is support for switches, firewalls, load balancers and WAAS appliances. The public elastic IP address (EIP) is assigned to a network interface and advertised across the internet. The EIP is a static public address that is persistent (remains assigned) even when the instance is stopped. The support for private and public addressing allows for subnetting and security zones. (A,C,E)

Question 29:

What is the difference between VPC main route table and custom route table?

A. VPC only creates a main route table when started

B. custom route table is the default

C. custom route table is created for public subnets

D. custom route table is created for private subnets

E. main route table is created for public and private subnets

Answer

The VPC creates a main route table as the default table. Any new subnet created after defining the VPC is associated with the main route table. It has a local route that is used for VPC routing between subnets. There is a route to the VPG gateway as well when attached. Tenants will configure a NAT instance for internet access instead of routing through the VPG gateway. The main route table should not have a route to the Internet gateway when it is associated with private subnets only. That exposes all private subnets to the internet.

The custom route table has a local route that is used for routing between subnets as well. In addition the tenant would add a default route to the Internet gateway. The tenant can associate a single or multiple subnets to the same custom route table. The best practice is to move all subnets that require internet access to a custom route table. The tenant must create a custom route table and associate the new public subnet to it. That will move the public subnet from the main route table and advertise the servers assigned to that subnet across the internet. That allows for control of VPC routing and optimizes security. (C)

Question 30:

What is the purpose of the native VPC router?

A. route packets across the internet

B. route packets between private cloud instances

C. route packets between subnets

D. route packets from instances to S3 storage volumes

E. route packets across VPN

Answer

The VPC router is the AWS native router assigned to each VPC that routes packets between subnets within the same VPC. Any packets destined for the internet are forwarded to the Internet gateway. In addition the VPC router is used for communicating between subnets, NAT, Internet gateway and virtual private gateway (VPG) when deployed. (C)

Question 31:

How are private DNS servers assigned to an Amazon VPC?

A. not supported

B. select nondefault VPC

C. select default VPC

D. select EC-2 classic

Answer

The nondefault VPC platform supports private DNS settings. That allows the company to assign the company domain name to EC2 instances. The tenant can configure a maximum of four enterprise DNS servers as well. That integrates the applications with on-premises DNS servers for server name resolution. DNS services are configured using AWS DHCP service options. (B)

Question 32:

What are two characteristics of an Amazon security group?

A. instance level packet filtering

B. deny rules only

C. permit rules only

D. subnet level packet filtering

E. inbound only

Answer

Amazon EC2 security groups are the equivalent of a static firewall for each VPC. They are provided by Amazon for instance level packet filtering. The security groups are comprised of multiple inbound and outbound permit rules assigned to each instance. There is a maximum of five security groups per instance and 100 security groups per VPC supported. There is no support for deny rules and reverse direction traffic is automatically permitted (stateful). The security group is associated with the EC2 instance to effect filtering. All rules are examined for a match before permitting or dropping packets. (A,C)

Question 33:

What statement is true of Network Access Control Lists (ACL) operation within an Amazon VPC?

A. instance and subnet level packet filtering

B. subnet level packet filtering

C. inbound only

D. only one ACL allowed per VPC

E. outbound only

Answer

This is an optional security feature available in addition to security groups for additional packet filtering. It is the second level of defense that supports allow and deny rules for subnets. Rules are applied to packets in a numbered order for matching purposes. The return traffic is inspected as well so it is stateless. (B)

Question 34:

How are packets forwarded between public and private subnets within VPC?

A. EIP

B. NAT

C. main route table

D. VPN

Answer

The public and private subnet model allows tenants to assign EC2 instances to public and private subnets. The public EC2 instances are assigned to a public subnet and private EC2 instances to a private subnet. That allows for deployment of application models with varying security requirements. The public EC2 instances are assigned a private IP address and public EIP address. That is used to advertise IP addressing across the internet. The tenant will attach a single Amazon Internet gateway to the VPC for public internet access.

The private EC2 instances are assigned private IP addressing. There are no incoming sessions allowed from the internet to the private subnets. The tenant can assign a NAT EC2 instance to a public subnet. That will forward traffic from private subnets to the Internet gateway for direct internet access. The private subnets can then connect to S3 storage and company software updates for instance. Any public EC2 instance without a public EIP address can use the NAT assigned EIP for internet access as well. (B)

Question 35:

What two statements accurately describe Amazon VPC architecture?

A. Elastic Load Balancer (ELB) cannot span multiple availability zones

B. VPC does not support DMVPN connection

C. VPC subnet cannot span multiple availability zones

D. VPC cannot span multiple regions

E. Flow logs are not supported within a VPC

Answer

Any single VPC must reside within the same region and subnets cannot span multiple availability zones. There is support for a single VPC or multiple VPC spanning multiple availability zones with Elastic Load Balancing between them. There is support for DMVPN with Cisco CSR 1000V routers instead of the native Amazon VPN Gateway and Flow Logs can be enabled per VPC. (C,D)

Question 36:

What is a requirement for attaching EC2 instances to on-premises clients and applications?

A. Amazon Virtual Private Gateway (VPN)

B. Amazon Internet Gateway

C. VPN Connection

D. Elastic Load Balancer (ELB)

E. NAT

Answer

Amazon AWS data center perimeter is comprised of internet routers and firewalls. They are physical appliance devices that connect to the Amazon switching infrastructure. Public IP addresses from multiple tenants is inspected at the internet edge routers. Amazon Internet gateways are available for connecting VPC public subnets to the internet and by extension on-premises clients and applications.

The tenant can connect with a variety of internet transport services including broadband services, MPLS and Metro Ethernet. The web servers EC2 instances are assigned to a VPC public subnet. The Internet gateway is required as well for public cloud services where VPC endpoints are not supported. There is only one Internet gateway assigned to each VPC. The Amazon perimeter devices inspect and forward packets to the tenant Internet gateway for any public IP (EIP) address assigned to the tenant. (B)

Question 37:

What two statements correctly describe Amazon Virtual private gateway?

A. assign to private subnets only

B. assign to public subnets only

C. single virtual private gateway per VPC

D. multiple virtual private gateways per VPC

E. single virtual private gateway per region

Answer

Amazon virtual private gateway (VPN) is assigned to the VPC private subnets. That provides a secure connection for the enterprise network and partners. The packets from the private subnets are forwarded to the VPG that has an assigned public internet address. That is used for connectivity to the VPN gateway at the tenant on-premises data center. There is only one virtual private gateway assigned to each VPC. AWS has a default feature that terminates VPN tunnels at redundant virtual private gateways located at different data centers. That enabled link redundancy and gateway redundancy for the same assigned VPC. (A,C)

Question 38:

What is the maximum access port speed available with Amazon Direct Connect service?

A. 1 Gbps

B. 10 Gbps

C. 500 Mbps

D. 100 Gbps

E. 100 Mbps

Answer

Amazon now offers Direct Connect for connecting enterprise data centers to applications in a VPC. The private WAN service is only available at Amazon AWS regional data centers. It is used for direct connectivity to an availability zone. The advantages of Direct Connect are security, performance and reliability with data center interconnectivity at 1 Gbps and 10 Gbps.

The increased bandwidth optimizes bulk data transfers from databases and delay sensitive traffic such as voice and video. The Direct Connect service is most suitable for companies with data centers near an Amazon AWS region data center. The circuit costs increase for data centers that are not near a region or APN partner. Inter-Region Direct Connect service is new and allows for connecting east and west regions. (B)

Question 39:

Refer to the topology drawing. Your company has asked you to configure a peering link between two VPCs that are currently not connected or exchanging any packets. What destination and target is configured in the routing table of VPC1 to enable packet forwarding to VPC2?

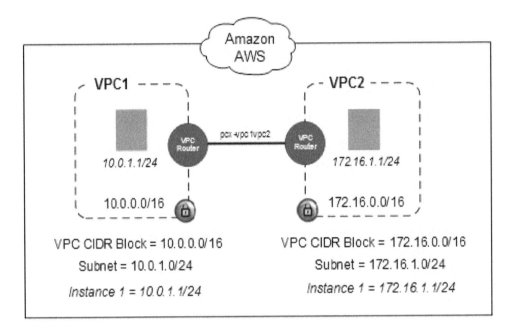

A. destination = 172.16.0.0/16
   target = pcx-vpc2vpc1

B. destination = 10.0.0.0/16
   target = pcx-vpc2

C. destination = 172.16.0.0/16
   target = 10.0.0.0/16

D. destination = 172.16.0.0/16
   target = pcx-vpc1vpc2

E. default route only

Answer

The VPC peering link (pcx-vpc1vpc2) requires a single route entry added to each VPC main route table. Any route entry is comprised of a destination and a target. The VPC1 routing table requires the following route. (D)

destination = 172.16.0.0/16
target = pcx-vpc1vpc2

Route Table: VPC1

Destination	*Target*
10.0.0.0/16	Local
172.16.0.0/16	pcx-vpc1vpc2

Route Table: VPC2

Destination	*Target*
172.16.0.0/16	Local
10.0.0.0/16	pcx-vpc1vpc2

Question 40:

How is routing enabled by default within a VPC for an EC2 instance?

A. add a default route

B. main route table

C. custom route table

D. must be configured explicitly

Answer

Amazon VPC often has multiple route tables and each instance is associated with the main route table or a custom route table. Amazon AWS assigns the subnet for an EC2 instance to the main route table as a default. As a result multiple subnets can be assigned to a route table. VPC routing within a VPC or peering is accomplished with the native VPC router assigned to each VPC.

Adding routes to any routing table for VPC peering requires the tenant to select the route table with the subnet assigned to an instance. Custom route tables are created by tenants for public subnets and Internet access for various purposes. The same subnet cannot be assigned to more than one route table. (B)

Question 41:

What three features are not supported with VPC peering?

A. overlapping CIDR blocks

B. IPv6 addressing

C. gateways

D. transitive routing

E. RedShift

Answer

Overlapping IP address ranges blocks are not permitted within a VPC. The design standard is to assign 10.0.0.0/16 CIDR block for instances assigned to private subnets. The tenant can use IP addresses from any private RFC 1918 address space. The tenant would typically use /24 subnet mask to subnet the third octet. This is an example of three non-overlapping subnets (10.0.1.0/24, 10.0.2.0/24, 10.0.3.0/24) assignable to a VPC.

Transitive routing occurs when a hub VPC is used to route packets between two connected spoke VPCs. That is not supported with Amazon AWS currently. Routing only occurs between directly connected VPCs. In addition Internet Gateways and VPN Gateways are not permitted in peering VPCs. They are not required either considering all traffic is within the Amazon AWS data centers whether it is the same or inter-region traffic. (A,C,D)

Question 42:

What route is used in a VPC routing table for packet forwarding to a Gateway?

A. static route

B. 10.0.0.0/16

C. 0.0.0.0/0

D. 0.0.0.0/16

Answer

All packets destined for the Internet Gateway or Virtual private gateway use route 0.0.0.0/0 (default route). (C)

Question 43:

You are asked to deploy a web application comprised of multiple public web servers with only private addressing assigned. What Amazon AWS solutions enables multiple servers on a private subnet with only a single EIP required and Availability Zone redundancy?

A. NAT instance

B. Internet gateway

C. Virtual private gateway

D. NAT gateway

E. Elastic Network Interface (ENI)

Answer

NAT Gateway decreases the number of Elastic IP addresses (public) required for an application with multiple public web servers to a single EIP. In addition there is support for redundancy with multiple NAT gateways assigned to separate Availability Zones. The tenant assigns a private (RFC 1918) IP address to each web server from the same subnet. That creates a private subnet with an associated route table that has no access to the internet. Add a NAT Gateway with an EIP to enable internet access. Add a default route to the routing table of web servers that points to the NAT Gateway.

The NAT Gateway is assigned to a public subnet and as a result has a custom route table. Add a default route to the custom route table of NAT Gateway that points to the Internet Gateway. The single EIP assigned to the NAT Gateway is used to enable internet access for all web servers on a private subnet. The Elastic Load Balancer (ELB) assigned to load balance inbound traffic from the internet to all web servers is assigned to the same public subnet as the NAT Gateway and by extension same custom route table. Outbound traffic from the web servers is first forwarded to ELB internal (private address). Each instance is assigned a private IP address for internal VPC routing whether or not it has a public interface. Inbound traffic from the internet is forwarded from the Internet Gateway to NAT Gateway where it is routed within VPC to ELB.

Traditional and cloud-based routing are vastly different. The traditional routers build a global routing table with all known subnets advertised from neighbors. The Amazon AWS cloud environment defines VPCs where each has multiple public and private route tables. Each subnet is associated with a separate route table. In addition one or multiple EC2 instances are associated with the route table for the subnet they are assigned. The VRF is a routing feature supported with enterprise routers that is somewhat similar to cloud routing tables. (D)

Question 44:

What is the IP addressing schema assigned to a default VPC?

A. 172.31.0.0/16 CIDR block subnetted with 172.31.0.0/20

B. 172.16.0.0/16 CIDR block subnetted with 172.16.0.0/24

C. 10.0.0.0/16 CIDR block subnetted with 10.0.0.0/24

D. 172.16.0.0/24 CIDR block subnetted with 172.31.0.0/18

Answer

Amazon AWS assigns 172.31.0.0/16 VPC CIDR block and further subnets it with 172.31.0.0/20 addressing. That subnets the third octet so that adding four new subnets on the bottom end of the range would include for instance 172.31.0.0/20, 172.31.16.0/20, 172.31.32.0/20 and 172.31.48.0/20 subnets. The first ten instances assigned to the first subnet (172.31.0.0/20) for example could be assigned 172.31.0.1/20 - 172.31.0.10/20 address range. The tenant would typically assign instances to multiple subnets based on network design, security and application requirements.

Tenants often select 10.0.0.0 private addressing as a result of its popularity and deployment for on-premises addressing. For example consider VPC CIDR block of 10.0.0.0/16 and Subnet CIDR block 10.0.0.0/24 (derived from VPC CIDR block) for creating multiple subnets. The first four IP addresses of any Subnet CIDR block are reserved for use by Amazon AWS. The instances assigned to the first available subnet (10.0.0.0/24) would start IP addressing for tenant instances at 10.0.0.5/24 address. The /24 subnet mask is used to subnet the 3rd octet of the CIDR block. (A)

    10.0.0.0 network address
    10.0.0.1 reserved for VPC router
    10.0.0.2 reserved for DNS services
    10.0.0.3 reserved
    10.0.0.255 broadcast address

The next subnet CIDR block available is 10.0.1.0/24 with the following reserved IP addresses:

    10.0.1.0 network address
    10.0.1.1 reserved for VPC router
    10.0.1.2 reserved for DNS services
    10.0.1.3 reserved
    10.0.1.255 broadcast address.

Question 45:

What default configuration and components are added by Amazon AWS when a tenant selects **Default VPC** type? (Select three)

A. Internet gateway

B. Virtual private gateway

C. NAT instance

D. security group

E. DNS

Answer

The default VPC is a starting point for tenants that enable basic services including internet access. The primary services include DNS, Internet Gateway, security groups and DHCP. The tenant would have configured DHCP settings previously from AWS console. There is a default security group and ACL associated with the default VPC type as well. All instances launched are assigned to the default security group. The tenant can modify any default configuration and create up to 100 security groups per VPC.

EC2 instances are initially assigned a public IPv4 address (not EIP) and a private IPv4 address. VPC instances support multiple Elastic Network Interfaces (ENI) where each ENI can be configured with a private and/or public IP address. The public IP address is released when EIP is assigned to the network interface. There is a default route (0.0.0.0/0) added to the main route table that forwards packets to the Internet Gateway. (A,D,E)

Question 46:

What feature requires tenants to disable source/destination check?

A. Elastic IP (EIP)

B. data replication

C. VPC peering

D. NAT

E. Internet gateway

Answer

EC2 instances perform source/destination check as a default setting. All EC2 instances must be the source or destination for any inbound or outbound packets. The NAT instance is a translation point where traffic transits between public and private subnets. As a result the tenant must disable source/destination check for the NAT instance. (D)

Storage Services

Question 1:

What AWS storage solution allows thousands of EC2 instances to simultaneously upload, access, delete and share files?

A. EBS

B. S3

C. Glacier

D. EFS

E. Storage Gateway

Answer

The recommended solution is Elastic File System (EFS) for enabling what is essentially a file server in the cloud. The EFS is associated with a single VPC where users with security permissions can access and share files. The Elastic File System is a managed service that is created and mounted on single or multiple Linux-based EC2 instances to enable data file storage and sharing. EFS provides file locking and strong consistency that is characteristic of a file system.

In addition EFS expands and shrinks based on when files are added or deleted. EBS storage is basically a hard drive volume attached to a single EC2 instance. It is used directly by servers for instance to run system files and store some application data. S3 is a publicly accessible service that stores objects of all sizes including logs for backup purposes. (D)

Figure 7 Elastic File System (EFS)

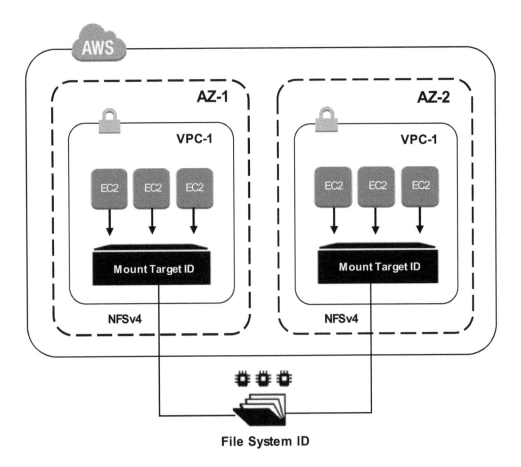

File System ID

Question 2:

What is required for an EFS mount target? (Select two)

A. EIP

B. DNS name

C. IP address

D. DHCP

E. IAM role

Answer

The mount target is a network interface used for communicating between multiple EC2 instances within an Availability Zone and EFS. The tenant would create a mount target in each Availability Zone for a region where tenants require access. The mount target IP address is assigned to the same subnet as the Availability Zone where EC2 instances reside. Where there are multiple subnets for EC2 instances, pick any one subnet for that Availability Zone.

The DNS name resolves the IP address when connecting to the EFS. There is no support currently for Inter-Region access of an EFS for tenants. You can access EFS from any Linux or Windows client that supports NFSv4. The current EFS architecture only supports Linux-based AMI (EC2 instances). The protocol used for communicating between EC2 and EFS is NFSv4. (B,C)

Question 3:

What connectivity features are recommended for copying on-premises files to EFS? (Select two)

A. VPN IPsec

B. Internet Gateway

C. Direct Connect

D. File Sync

E. FTP

F. AWS Storage Gateway

Answer

The fastest method for copying on-premises files to EFS is with Direct Connect and File Sync. Amazon AWS recommends Direct Connect for high throughput low latency connections between on-premises and AWS cloud services. It is a private connection that when used in concert with File Sync provides best performance when copying large files frequently. It is the most costly option available as well. Direct Connect allows tenants to mount an EFS file system from on-premises where files can be moved between servers for various applications. It is commonly referred to as a hybrid cloud where at least one server for an application resides on-premises. The advantage of File Sync is that is can copy on-premises files across any network connection to AWS cloud. It is 5x faster than standard Linux tools and data is encrypted in transit with integrity checks on the link. (C,D)

Question 4:

What AWS services encrypts data at rest as a default feature? (Select two)

A. S3

B. AWS Storage Gateway

C. EBS

D. Glacier

E. RDS

Answer

Most AWS services require tenants to select some encryption technique when it is available. It is typically a choice of client-side or server-side encryption that determines key management and tenant responsibility. In addition there is support for in-transit and data at rest encryption for data security. Only AWS Storage Gateway and Glacier provide native encryption of data. (B,D)

Question 5:

What fault tolerant features are supported for S3 storage? (Select three)

A. cross-region replication

B. versioning must be disabled

C. cross-region asynchronous replication of objects

D. synchronous replication of objects within a region

E. multiple destination buckets

Answer

Amazon AWS creates S3 buckets in a region by default. The bucket names are globally unique and lowercase. Cross-region replication is supported for S3 buckets to enable optimized fault tolerance for tenant data. It is a bucket-level configuration on the source bucket that provides automatic asynchronous copying of objects across buckets to different AWS Regions. The source bucket and destination bucket can be owned by the same or different AWS accounts. There is only support for cross-region replication to a single bucket. The tenant must enable versioning on buckets. In addition S3 must have permissions to replicate objects from source to destination bucket.

That is enabled with security access granted through an IAM created role for S3 replication feature. Object replicas are stored using the same storage class as the source object, unless modified in the replication configuration. Note as well that replicas have the same key names and metadata. Amazon replicates each object synchronously to three Availability Zones within a region by default as well. (A,C,D)

Question 6:

What is the fastest technique for deleting 900 objects in an S3 bucket with a single HTTP request?

A. Multi-Part Delete API

B. Multi-Object Delete API

C. 100 objects is maximum per request

D. Fast-Delete API

Answer

Amazon S3 provides the Multi-Object Delete API that you can use to delete up to 1000 objects in a single HTTP request. (B)

Question 7:

What security controls technique is recommended for S3 cross-account access?

A. IAM group

B. security groups

C. S3 ACL

D. bucket policies

Answer

IAM policies are recommended where there are numerous buckets with complex permissions. AWS S3 bucket policies are the preferred solution for cross-account access. (D)

Question 8:

What are two advantages of cross-region replication of an S3 bucket?

A. cost

B. security compliance

C. scalability

D. Beanstalk support

E. minimize latency

Answer

Storing S3 data in multiple Availability Zones and Regions is sometime required for security compliance of an application. In addition cross-region access minimizes latency for customers and employees located in different regions. The same is true of AWS services in two different regions accessing S3 data. (B,E)

Question 9:

What are two primary difference between Amazon S3 Standard and S3/RRS storage classes?

A. Amazon Standard does not replicate at all

B. RRS provides higher durability

C. RRS provides higher availability

D. RRS does not replicate objects as many times

E. application usage is different

Answer

Amazon Standard storage class provides 99.999999999% durability and availability for objects. It is designed and recommended for frequently accessed data associated with cloud application and web hosting. There is multiple replication deployed that enables high availability across multiple facilities. Amazon Reduced Redundancy Storage (RRS) provides only 99.99% durability and availability to objects. It is recommended only for dynamic, temporary and reproducible content. Tenants often have the same content durably stored somewhere else as well.

There is much less replication and can only sustain loss of data in a single facility. Amazon S3 Standard Infrequent Access as the name suggests is similar to Standard however it is recommended for less frequently accessed data such as backups. (D,E)

Question 10:

What two features are enabled with S3 services?

A. store objects of any size

B. dynamic web content

C. supports Provisioned IOPS

D. store virtually unlimited amounts of data

E. bucket names are globally unique

Answer

S3 does have an object file size limit of 5 TB however there is no limit on the number of objects (virtually unlimited). There is no support for provisioned IOPS (databases only) or support for dynamic web content. Tenants can only deploy static web content to S3 storage. The bucket names are globally unique and lowercase with a default of only 100 per account. (D,E)

Question 11:

What new feature was recently added to SQS that defines how messages are ordered?

A. streams

B. SNS

C. FIFO

D. TLS

E. decoupling

Answer

First-in First-out (FIFO) queuing orders messages in the queue based on when they arrive. It is called sequencing and a feature required by some applications for processing messages. The standard queueing operation stores all messages with best-effort ordering only. There is a maximum of 300 transactions/sec. supported with a single FIFO queue. (C)

Question 12:

What two AWS storage types are persistent?

A. ephemeral

B. S3

C. EBS

D. instance store

E. SAML

Answer

Any persistent storage associated with an EC2 instance is not deleted when the instance is stopped or terminated. Ephemeral and instance store are temporary working storage that is deleted when the instance is stopped. Amazon automatically replicates EBS volumes as well within the same Availability Zone.

The tenant selects the Amazon Machine Image (AMI) associated with an instance to launch it. The root device volume for an EC2 instance contains the image used to boot the instance. The options for root devices include AMI backed by Amazon EC2 instance store or AMI backed by Amazon EBS. Instance store is not persistent and slower than the recommended EBS. Note that EBS storage and the EC2 instance must reside in the same availability zone and by extension region. (B,C)

Question 13:

Select three on-premises backup solutions used for copying data to an Amazon AWS S3 bucket?

A. AWS Import/Export

B. RDS

C. Snowball

D. Availability Zone (AZ) replication

E. AWS Storage Gateway

Answer

The primary on-premises solutions for data backups to S3 buckets are AWS Import/Export, Snowball and Storage Gateway. The cost, speed and recovery time is what differentiates the services. The other options are not part of any on-premises backup solution to AWS. Direct Connect is a high speed private cloud link that is available as well for copying large amounts of data. (A,C,E)

Question 14:

You have 1 TB of data and want to archive the data that won't be accessed that often. What Amazon AWS storage solution is recommended?

A. Glacier

B. EBS

C. ephemeral

D. CloudFront

Answer

Amazon Glacier is a cost effective cloud storage solution used mostly for archiving data. The tenant can use it to backup data from S3 buckets as well for additional data redundancy or for data that isn't accessed that frequently. The tenant can use Amazon Import/Export that supports transferring on-premises data to portable storage devices. The portable devices are then shipped to Amazon support engineers where data is copied to S3 buckets and/or Glacier vaults. It is more cost effective and faster than data transfer across the internet for bulk data. (A)

Question 15:

What are three methods of accessing DynamoDB for customization purposes?

A. CLI

B. AWS console

C. API call

D. vCenter

E. Beanstalk

Answer

Amazon AWS has enabled three primary methods for tenant to access, provision and configure a variety of services. They include AWS console with GUI, command line interface (CLI) and API calls. (A,B,C)

Question 16:

What are two primary differences between Glacier and S3 storage services?

A. Glacier is lower cost

B. S3 is lower cost

C. Glacier is preferred for frequent data access with lower latency

D. S3 is preferred for frequent data access with lower latency

E. S3 supports larger file size

Answer

S3 is used for storing frequently accessed data with faster low latency performance. There is a high cost associated with S3 however it is scalable, easy and multi-purpose. S3 data typically include EBS snapshots, bulk storage, low cost internet storage (Dropbox) and public web server data. In addition instance store volume when selected is created from a template stored on S3 bucket. EBS is preferred today for EC2 instances with faster performance and persistent store. (A,D)

Question 17:

What statement correctly describes the operation of AWS Glacier archive?

A. archive is a group of vaults

B. archive is an unencrypted vault

C. archive supports aggregated files only

D. maximum file size is 1 TB

E. archive supports single and aggregated files

Answer

Data is stored in Amazon Glacier storage service as files called archives. There is support for single file or aggregating multiple files to a single TAR or ZIP file. The total volume of data and number of archives you can store are unlimited. Amazon AWS charges less when files are aggregated and maximum file size is 40 TB archive. Vault is a file management feature where archives can be assigned to the same or different vaults. Amazon supports grouping of archives and adding vault-level security policies through Identity and Access Management (IAM). There is a notification service as well per vault that alerts tenants when files are ready for download. (E)

Question 18:

What are three primary differences between S3 vs EBS?

A. S3 is a multi-purpose public internet-based storage

B. EBS is directly assigned to a tenant VPC EC2 instance

C. EBS and S3 provide persistent storage

D. EBS snapshots are typically stored on S3 buckets

E. EBS and S3 use buckets to manage files

Answer

EBS is similar to a traditional hard drive that uses block level storage and requires formatting a file system. It is directly assigned to a single EC2 instance for persistent storage and fast. EBS volume snapshots are easy to create and store on S3 buckets. In addition you can create AMI from an EBS snapshot.

That allows you to modify and save a new AMI for some different usage. S3 is an internet-based multi-purpose storage solution used as a repository for data. It is an easier object- oriented storage service that supports data from multiple sources. In addition S3 is lower cost designed for fault tolerance (redundancy) and scalability. It is popular as a backup solutions of on-premises data from enterprise data centers. Note that data encryption is supported with both EBS and S3 for optimized security. The following are examples of data types that use S3 buckets as a store. (A,B,D)

- EBS Snapshots
- On-Premises Backups
- CloudFront Content
- Bulk Data
- Multi-Region Access
- Database storage (RDS, RedShift etc)

Question 19:

What on-premises solution is available from Amazon AWS to minimize latency for all data?

A. Gateway-VTL

B. Gateway-cached volumes

C. Gateway-stored volumes

D. EBS

E. S3 bucket

F. ElastiCache

Answer

Amazon AWS Storage Gateway is a hybrid solution that supports storing some or all data on-premises for faster performance. The Gateway is a software (virtual) appliance that is deployed on-premises (enterprise data center). The Gateway-stored volume option stores data for all applications on-premises. That minimizes latency and provides the fastest response time available when compared with cloud-based storage. Amazon AWS takes regular snapshots of the data and backup to S3 bucket for disaster recovery purposes. The other options are Gateway-cached and Gateway-VTL that store some or all data in the cloud. (C)

Question 20:

What feature transitions S3 storage to Standard-IA for cost optimization?

A. RRS/S3

B. Glacier vault

C. storage class analysis

D. path-based routing

Answer

The purpose of storage class analysis is to analyze storage access patterns and transition selected data to the best storage class. It is an S3 analytical tool that automatically identifies infrequent access patterns and transitions data to S3 Standard-Infrequent Access (IA). The tenant must configure storage class analysis policies to enable bucket monitoring. The policies also support monitoring and analysis based on S3 prefix or object tag. (C)

Question 21:

How does AWS uniquely identify S3 objects?

A. bucket name

B. version

C. key

D. object tag

Answer

An S3 object is comprised of object data and metadata. The metadata is a set of name-value pairs that describe the object including some default metadata, such as the date last modified, and Content-Type. The unique identifier for each S3 object in a bucket is an assigned key.

The S3 object is addressed using a bucket name + key + optional version ID. The attributes are used to create a URL that uniquely identifies the object for access. The web services endpoint includes the region where the object is located as well a part of the URL. (C)

Question 22:

What is the advantage of read-after-write consistency for S3 buckets?

A. no stale reads for PUT of any new object in all regions

B. higher throughput for all requests

C. stale reads for PUT requests in some regions

D. no stale reads for GET requests in a single regions

Answer

The PUT operation is used by a web-based application to create or update (write operations) an object to an S3 bucket. In addition S3 synchronously replicates the data to multiple Availability Zones. The advantage of read-after-write consistency is no stale reads for PUT of new objects. Any user that makes a read (GET) request for the objects will have the most updated version.

It is a key aspect of any storage or database service to return updated data immediately based on a user request. S3 now provides read-after-write consistency for all AWS regions as well. There is eventual consistency for overwrite PUT and DELETE operations that sometimes returns stale data however there is somewhat lower latency and higher throughput. (A)

Question 23:

What is the maximum single file object size supported with Amazon S3?

A. 5 GB

B. 5 TB

C. 1 TB

D. 100 GB

Answer

AWS S3 supports a single file object size of 5 TB however it requires Multipart Upload API feature to upload in 5 GB increments. Amazon AWS S3 is an internet-based storage service that requires an internet gateway for tenant access. The architecture defines objects of up to 5 TB in size. Objects are assigned to buckets and buckets are assigned to availability zones. In addition buckets can be assigned to multiple availability zones for failover and load balancing.

Bucket is a container that has one or multiple objects assigned. The tenant is assigned a key to retrieve files. There is unlimited capacity, data encryption and security rights assignable to data. Amazon assigns and stores a bucket to an availability zone. The availability zone is a data center assigned to a region. There are multiple designated AWS regions around the world. Select the region for your availability zone/s where latency is minimized for primary and redundant connections. The AWS regions are selectable based on tenant location and services availability. (B)

Question 24:

What security problem is solved by Cross-Origin Resource Sharing (CORS)?

A. enable HTTP requests from within scripts to a different domain

B. enable sharing of web-based files between different buckets

C. provide security for third party objects within AWS

D. permits sharing objects between AWS services

Answer

For security reasons making HTTP requests (GET, PUT etc.) from within scripts (Java) is not permitted to a different domain (cross-domains) than the source domain where the web browser originated the request. CORS permits S3 bucket as an origin to forward requests. You can create an XML file with up to 100 rules and permit all origins to access objects in a bucket. S3 after receiving a preflight request from the web browser sends it to an XML file. CORS must be enabled on HTTP endpoints that connect to an API gateway for RESTful APIs. (A)

Question 25:

What is recommended for migrating 40 TB of data from on-premises to AWS S3 when the internet link is often over utilized?

A. AWS Storage gateway

B. AWS Snowball

C. AWS Import/Export

D. AWS Elastic File System

E. AWS Elasticsearch

Answer

The recommended solution for moving a large amount of on-premises data to the AWS cloud as fast as possible is AWS Snowball. It is an appliance-based storage device shipped to the tenant where up to 50 TB of data can be loaded. The appliance is shipped back to the tenant where AWS receives it and copies data over to AWS S3 storage.

There is support for multiple appliances with concurrent data transfers as well as 256-bit encryption on data at rest for security purposes. Snowball is preferred now as a replacement for AWS Import/Export particularly with larger data transfers. The tenant creates a job in the AWS Management Console and a Snowball appliance is automatically shipped on-premises. (B)

Question 26:

Your company is publishing an online catalog of books that is currently using DynamoDB for storing the information associated with each item. There is a requirement to add images for each book. What solution is most cost effective and designed for that purpose?

A. RedShift

B. EBS

C. RDS

D. S3

E. Kinesis

Answer

DynamoDB is a one-dimensional data structure that stores a large amount of information. It is based on store and lookup and doesn't support the complex queries associated with relational databases (RDS, Aurora etc). There is however an item limit of 400 KB that is often less than what is required for images. S3 is designed to store objects up to 5 GB per PUT and 5 TB maximum size that is cost effective and with low latency. (D)

Question 27:

You have an application that collects monitoring data from 10,000 sensors (IoT) deployed in the USA. The datapoints are comprised of video events for home security and environment status alerts. The application will be deployed to AWS with EC2 instances as data collectors. What AWS storage service is preferred for storing video files from sensors?

A. RedShift

B. RDS

C. S3

D. DynamoDB

Answer

IoT sensors that deliver video events require larger file size storage and fewer considering it is event-based when a security alert occurs. Amazon S3 is well suited for storing fewer larger files (videos) as objects when deploying an IOT solution. In addition there is lifecycle management where data can be migrated to Glacier vaults. (C)

Security Architecture

Question 1:

What statements correctly describe security groups within a VPC? (Select three)

A. default security group only permit inbound traffic

B. security groups are stateful firewalls

C. only allow rules are supported

D. allow and deny rules are supported

E. security groups are associated to network interfaces

Answer

Security groups are associated with a network interface assigned to an EC2 instance. There is support for multiple allow rules that can be configured to filter inbound and outbound packets. The default security group permits all inbound and outbound traffic between all instances. EC2 instances cannot communicate when a new security group replaces the default group unless rules are added to explicitly permit it. The unconfigured security group explicitly denies all inbound and outbound traffic. The operational mode is stateful so that any security group rules permitting an inbound session also permit outbound traffic for the same session by default. (B,C,E)

Question 2:

What three items are required to configure a security group rule?

A. protocol type

B. VPC name

C. port number

D. source IP

E. destination IP

F. description

Answer

AWS security group rules are comprised of source IP, protocol type and port range. Add a description to the security group for troubleshooting. (A,C,D)

- protocol type = TCP, UDP, ICMP, All etc.
- port number = single port or multiple (range) of application ports
- source = individual IPv4 address, IPv6 address or destination security group

Question 3:

What two source IP address types are permitted in a security group rule?

A. only CIDR blocks with /16 subnet mask

B. source IP address 0.0.0.0/0

C. single source IP address with /24 subnet mask

D. security group id

E. IPv6 address with /64 prefix length

Answer

All EC2 instances associated with a security group are affected by any changes to the permit rules. There are separate tables within a security group for inbound and outbound rules. There is support for single source IP address with /32 subnet mask, CIDR block range, all source IP addresses (0.0.0.0/0) and a security group id. The tenant can deploy IPv6 addressing to a VPC however AWS security groups only support prefix-length of /128 for single IPv6 address.

The following example permits SSH (22) and HTTPS (443) from 200.200.1.1/32 source public address. That could be the public address of a connection from the enterprise data center. In addition HTTP and ICMP (Ping) are permitted from all source IP addresses (0.0.0.0/0). (B,D)

Inbound Rules

Protocol Type	Port Number	Source IP
TCP	22	200.200.1.1/32
TCP	443	200.200.1.1/32
TCP	80	0.0.0.0/0
ICMP	ALL	0.0.0.0/0

Question 4:

What protocols must be enabled for remote access to Linux-based and Windows-based EC2 instances?

A. SSH, ICMP, Telnet

B. SSH, HTTP, RDP

C. SSH, HTTP, SSL

D. SSH, RDP, ICMP

Answer

Amazon AWS supports both Linux-based AMI and Windows-based AMI from various on-premises hypervisors. The security group rules assigned to EC2 instances must be updated to enable inbound SSH (Linux), RDP (Windows), and ICMP access. That permits tenant access to EC2 instances from the enterprise data center. ICMP packets are enabled for routing management traffic and Ping command. (D)

Question 5:

What features distinguish Network ACLs from security groups within a VPC? (Select three)

A. ACL filters at the subnet level

B. ACL is based on deny rules only

C. ACL is applied to instances and subnets

D. ACL is stateless

E. ACL supports a numbered list for filtering

Answer

Network ACL is a stateless security service that is configured and assigned to a VPC subnet. There are allow and deny rules supported for inbound and outbound tables per ACL. In addition you can assign the same single ACL across multiple subnets however only one ACL per subnet. Each subnet must be assigned to an ACL. The default ACL is assigned and permits all inbound and outbound IPv4 and IPv6 traffic unless a new ACL is assigned. The ACL is evaluated based on a defined order called a number or sequence list. (A,D,E)

Question 6:

What happens to the security permissions of a tenant when an IAM role is granted? (Select two)

A. tenant inherits only permissions assigned to the IAM role temporarily

B. add security permissions of the IAM role to existing permissions

C. previous security permissions are no longer in effect

D. previous security permissions are deleted unless reconfigured

E. tenant inherits only read permissions assigned to the IAM role

Answer

The IAM role grants temporary permission to a user or application for some specific purpose. Any permission the role grants do not add to the permissions already granted to the user or application. When there is a role switch any previous permissions are dropped in exchange for permissions granted with the new role. The previous (original) permissions are automatically restored when the role is removed from user or application. (A,C)

Question 7:

Where are IAM permissions granted to invoke and execute a Lambda function for S3 access? (Select two)

A. S3 bucket

B. EC2 instance

C. Lambda function

D. IAM role

E. event mapping

Answer

The event source mapping is configured to associate a source event with a Lambda function. The Lambda function defined in the bucket notification configuration is triggered when an event is detected such as a user copying a file to an S3 bucket. The Lambda function verifies security permissions before executing it on AWS services. (A,D)

96

The S3 bucket is the event source that must be granted permissions to invoke the Lambda function. In addition the IAM role permissions you assigned to Lambda when the function was created is inherited by the Lambda function. The role permissions must allow access to the S3 bucket to run the function.

Question 8:

You have some developers working on code for an application and they require temporary access to AWS cloud up to an hour. What is the easiest web-based solution from AWS to provides access and minimize security exposure?

A. ACL

B. security group

C. IAM group

D. STS

E. EFS

Answer

AWS Security Token Service (AWS STS) enables trusted users with temporary security credentials to access AWS services. That could include existing IAM users that have permanent security credentials or temporary users that do not. The intent is to allow access for up to hour by default and then revoke access.

Any new access required would require a new STS request for the user. The advantage is the security access is not stored, does not become part of any application configuration or AWS security schema. The user can request new credentials, as long as the user requesting them still has permissions to do so at or before the expiry time. The US east-region is default for requesting STS services however multiple regions are supported. (D)

Question 9:

What two methods are used to request temporary credentials based on AWS Security Token Service (STS)?

A. Web Identity Federation

B. LDAP

C. IAM identity

D. dynamic ACL

E. private key rotation

Answer

IAM registered users have existing security permission based on granted access to AWS. User with an existing IAM identity and associated security credentials are granted temporary access through IAM. The temporary user with no existing IAM identity account are authenticated from an external on-premises federated store with SAML for Single Sign-on. The user makes a request for AWS access that is forwarded to an on-premises identity provider.

The IdP then authenticates user credentials to an identity store (LDAP, ADS etc) and generates a SAML security token. The security token is forwarded to AWS STS via *AssumeRoleWithSAML* API call. The API returns credentials for the temporary session to the user. They consist of an access key ID, secret access key and security session token. The permissions to access AWS services are granted as a result through private Federated identity.

There is Web Identity Federation as well where credentials from well-known supported platforms such as Facebook and Google are used to access AWS services. Web Federated Identity does not require distribution of access keys either for added security. (A,C)

Figure 8 AWS Security Token Service with SAML Federation

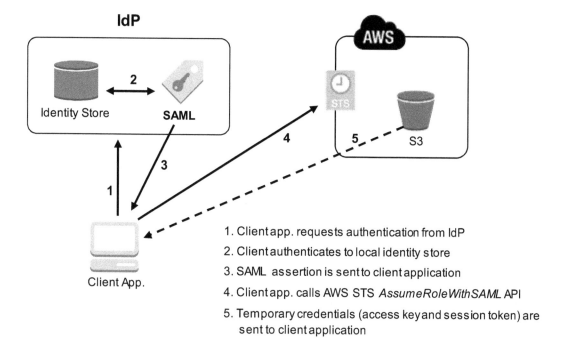

1. Client app. requests authentication from IdP
2. Client authenticates to local identity store
3. SAML assertion is sent to client application
4. Client app. calls AWS STS *AssumeRoleWithSAML* API
5. Temporary credentials (access key and session token) are sent to client application

Question 10:

What two components are required for enabling SAML authentication requests to AWS Identity and Access Management (IAM)?

A. access keys

B. session token

C. SSO

D. identity provider (IdP)

E. SAML provider entity

Answer

Tenants must configure a SAML identity provider (IdP) that sends claims required by AWS security schema. In addition IAM is used to create a SAML provider entity in your AWS account that represents your identity provider and create an IAM role that specifies you as a SAML provider in its trust policy. (D,E)

Question 11:

What are two reasons for deploying Origin Access Identity (OAI) when enabling CloudFront?

A. prevent users from deleting objects in S3 buckets

B. mitigate distributed denial of service attacks (DDoS)

C. prevent users from accessing objects with Amazon S3 URL

D. prevent users from accessing objects with CloudFront URL

E. replace IAM for internet-based customer authentication

Answer

The purpose of Origin Access Identity (OAI) is to prevent users from accessing any S3 content (objects) with Amazon S3 URLs. It is a solution particularly applicable where HTTP servers are deployed for a web-based application. The following steps are required by tenants to enable OAI for their application.

1. Create a special CloudFront user called an origin access identity from the CloudFront console or API.

2. Give the origin access identity permission to read the objects in your bucket. The user account is a proxy for all user access and retrieves objects for them.

3. Remove permissions for users to access Amazon S3 URLs to read objects. The user is denied access to objects based on an Amazon S3 URL and cannot bypass CloudFront security or infrastructure.

In addition to CloudFront security, OAI also mitigates the effects of any distributed denial of service attack (DDoS). SYN floods are a common DDoS that exploit the TCP three-way handshake. Any user requests are forwarded through CloudFront (and AWS) security where there is security enabled instead of S3 public access endpoints. That minimizes the attack surface to a private security managed infrastructure. (B,C)

Question 12:

What solutions are recommended to mitigate DDoS attacks? (Select three)

A. host-based firewall

B. elastic load balancer

C. WAF

D. SSL/TLS

E. Bastion host

F. NAT gateway

Answer

The most common strategies for mitigating DDoS attacks include horizontal scaling, redundancy, minimize attack surface, limit source IP addresses and packet inspection. Amazon AWS Elastic Load Balancer with Auto-Scaling architecture enables horizontal scaling to add capacity allowing time to detect and mitigate. WAF (Web Application Firewall) is integrated with CloudFront and can detect DDoS request traffic patterns with web ACLs and mitigate attacks. Bastion host whitelist of IP addresses denies traffic from sources not approved. (B,C,E)

Question 13:

What features are required to prevent users from bypassing AWS CloudFront security? (Select three)

A. Bastion host

B. signed URL

C. IP whitelist

D. signed cookies

E. origin access identity (OAI)

Answer

The features that prevent users from bypassing CloudFront (and by extension AWS) security is CloudFront signed URLs and signed cookies. The private content in S3 buckets is accessed with CloudFront URLs provided to select users. The signed attributes include restrictions for users as part of defined security requirements. That permits security controls on content permitted by select users and charges where applicable. One part of a signed URL or cookie is hashed and signed using the private key from a public/private key pair.

CloudFront compares the signed and unsigned portions of the URL or cookie provided by the user to grant access. The request is denied when they do not match. Origin Access Identity is required as well to prevent users from accessing objects in an HTTP server. CloudFront supports a variety of origin servers and custom origin servers often as part of a content solution. HTTP server is a custom origin server with objects that must be publicly accessible. As a result public objects are available to anyone who has the object URL without logging on or paying for the content. The purpose of OAI is to prevent unauthorized users from accessing objects with an S3 (public) URL. (B,D,E)

Question 14:

What is the advantage of resource-based policies for cross-account access?

A. trusted account permissions are not replaced

B. trusted account permissions are replaced

C. resource-based policies are easier to deploy

D. trusting account manages all permissions

Answer

The trusted account permissions granted to the tenant are not replaced when resource-based security policies are deployed. The resource that you want to share must support resource-based policies. The resource-based policy is comprised of AWS account ID numbers that can access a resource. Role permissions replace any tenant account permission they were granted with the trusted account with the trusting account. Tenant retains all security permissions from trusted and trusting account that were granted when resource-based policies are used. (A)

Question 15:

Select three requirements for configuring a Bastion host?

A. EIP

B. SSH inbound permission

C. default route

D. CloudWatch logs group

E. VPN

F. Auto-Scaling

Answer

The purpose of a Bastion host is to provide a security zone between a public subnet and private subnet to minimize the attack surface. It is a proxy that prevents direct access for SSH/RDP connections from the internet to private subnet EC2 instances. As a result tenants can access and manage EC2 instances through the Bastion host. The following lists the requirements for deploying a Bastion host for SSH only. (A,B,D)

- Bastion host deployed to each public subnet
- Security group assigned to Bastion host instance with SSH inbound allowed
- Network ACL with SSH inbound and outbound allowed
- NAT instance to forward packets from public subnet to private subnet.

Question 16:

What rule must be added to the security group assigned to a mount target instance that enables EFS access from an EC2 instance?

A. Type = EC2, protocol = IP, port = 2049, source = remote security group

B. Type = EC2, protocol = EFS, port = 2049, source = 0.0.0.0/0

C. Type = NFS, protocol = TCP, port = 2049, source = remote security group

D. Type = NFSv4, protocol = UDP, port = 2049, source = remote security group

Answer

Allowing access between EC2 instance and mount target instance requires the tenant to modify the security groups assigned to each so the traffic flow is permitted. The source is the security group ID of the EC2 instance. The tenant must the following rule to the security group that is assigned to the mount target instance. (C)

Type = NFS, protocol = TCP, port = 2049, source = sg-3456scde

Question 17:

What statement correctly describes IAM architecture?

A. IAM security is unified per region and replicated based on requirements for an AWS tenant account

B. IAM security is defined per region for roles only on an AWS tenant account

C. IAM security is globally unified across the AWS cloud for an AWS tenant account

D. IAM security is defined separately per region and cross-region security enabled for an AWS tenant account

Answer

Identity and Access Management (IAM) is the security schema that defines access to AWS resources for each tenant that and associated AWS account/s. Each tenant has multiple users that require various security access to AWS services. The IAM defines users, groups and roles to create granular security permissions based on security access requirements. IAM security is globally unified across the AWS cloud for an AWS tenant account.

The tenant does not have to create new roles for instance in different regions or Availability Zones. It is unified globally where existing groups and roles can be assigned, modified or added based on requirements. (C)

Question 18:

What are two advantages of customer-managed encryption keys (CMK)?

A. create and rotate encryption keys

B. AES-128 cipher for data at rest

C. audit encryption keys

D. encrypts data in-transit for server-side encryption only

Answer

AWS KMS service allows you to create, rotate, delete, disable and audit Customer Master Key (CMK) encryption keys from the IAM console. It provides centralized control over encryption and decryption of data based on defined IAM policies for users, roles and cross-account access to use a CMK. There is integration with CloudTrail as well to audit all CMK usage transactions for security compliance requirements. (A,C)

Question 19:

What feature is not available with AWS Trusted Advisor?

A. cost optimization

B. infrastructure best practices

C. vulnerability assessment

D. monitor application metrics

Answer

Amazon Inspector is a security assessment service from AWS that scans tenant infrastructure for security vulnerabilities and makes recommendations. That is based on known current vulnerabilities with applications for example. Trusted Advisor is used for cost optimization in addition to advising tenants on best practices for performance optimization and security. (C)

Question 20:

What is required to Ping from a source instance to a destination instance?

A. Network ACL: not required
   Security Group: allow ICMP outbound on source/destination EC2 instances

B. Network ACL: allow ICMP inbound/outbound on source/destination subnets
   Security Group: not required

C. Network ACL: allow ICMP inbound/outbound on source/destination subnets
   Security Group: allow ICMP outbound on source EC2 instance
   Security Group: allow ICMP inbound on destination EC2 instance

D. Network ACL: allow TCP inbound/outbound on source/destination subnets
   Security Group: allow TCP and ICMP inbound on source EC2 instance

Answer

The source EC2 instance requires a security group with an outbound rule allowing ICMP. The destination EC2 instance requires a security group with an inbound rule allowing ICMP. In addition ICMP must be allowed inbound and outbound for the network ACL on each subnet where the instances are assigned. Subnets cannot span Availability Zones so there are two separate subnets and network ACLs. (C)

- Network ACL: allow ICMP inbound and outbound on both subnets
- Security Group: allow ICMP outbound on source EC2 instance
- Security Group: allow ICMP inbound on destination EC2 instance

Question 21:

What two steps are required in order to grant cross-account permissions between AWS accounts?

A. create an IAM user

B. attach a trust policy to S3

C. create a transitive policy

D. attach a trust policy to the role

E. create an IAM role

Answer

You can attach an identity-based permissions policy to an IAM role to grant cross-account permissions. The purpose of an IAM role is to grant permission to a user, AWS service or application. The role is a defined set of policies that permit access to an AWS resource. For example a database administrator could grant cross-account permissions to a developer in account APPDEV. The access would allow the developer to copy data to an S3 bucket owned by the database administrator. The following steps are required for granting cross-account permission to an S3 bucket. (D,E)

1. The database administrator creates an IAM role and assigns APPDEV account to it.

2. The database administrator attaches a permissions policy to the role that grants permissions for account APPDEV to access S3 bucket.

3. The database administrator attaches a trust policy to the role identifying account APPDEV as the principal who can assume the role.

Question 22:

You have configured a security group to allow ICMP, SSH and RDP inbound and assigned the security group to all instances in a subnet. There is no access to any Linux-based or Windows-based instances and you cannot Ping any instances. The network ACL for the subnet is configured to allow all inbound traffic to the subnet. What is the most probable cause?

A. on-premises firewall rules

B. security group and network ACL outbound rules

C. network ACL outbound rules

D. security group outbound rules

E. Bastion host required

F. WAF filtering required

Answer

The fact that inbound rules are configured on the security group would point to the network ACL outbound rules as the problem. Security groups are stateful meaning allowing traffic inbound is all that is required. The same security group will automatically allow the same inbound traffic outbound as well.

The network ACL is stateless so that inbound rules will require matching outbound rules for a subnet where the instance resides. It isn't enough to allow inbound traffic only for the protocols. The default network ACL for each subnet allows all traffic so that customizing it would deny inbound and outbound rules unless explicitly granted. (C)

Question 23:

What three techniques provide authentication security on S3 volumes?

A. bucket policies

B. network ACL

C. Identity and Access Management (IAM)

D. encryption

E. AES256

Answer

The tenant should configure data and file security to S3 volumes based on requirements. The user authentication method is based on bucket policies, ACLs and query strings. Amazon AWS Identity and Access Management features allow administrators to manage and assign storage security permissions to user groups. (A,B,C)

Question 24:

What statement correctly describes support for AWS encryption of S3 objects?

A. tenants manage encryption for server-side encryption of S3 objects

B. Amazon manages encryption for server-side encryption of S3 objects

C. client-side encryption of S3 objects is not supported

D. S3 buckets are encrypted only

E. SSL is only supported with Glacier storage

Answer

Amazon AWS manage all aspects of server-side encryption for S3 objects. The objects are encrypted and decrypted on the S3 volume. Client-side encryption (data in transit) is supported as well however it is managed by tenants. In addition there is SSL available for client-side encryption to AWS cloud. (B)

Question 25:

What authentication method provides Federated Single Sign-On (SSO) for cloud applications?

A. ADS

B. ISE

C. RADIUS

D. TACACS

E. SAML

Answer

Security Assertion Markup Language (SAML) is used to authorize access to SAML-enabled SaaS applications after network authentication is approved. The SaaS applications have additional security that authorize specific features and data access. The tenant can use LDAP or SAML for directory services and application security. SAML is more suited to cloud applications with additional features that improve security and ease management.

SAML enables federated Single Sign-On (SSO) to integrate authentication and authorization for end users. Single Sign-On authorizes a user to all applications instead of having to sign-on to multiple servers and services. SAML has many advantages compared with LDAP for cloud-based SaaS applications. The SaaS management portal allow tenants to configure stringent password policies. That provides optimized security for tenant application and database security compliance. (E)

Question 26:

Based on the AWS security model, what infrastructure configuration and associated security is the responsibility of tenants and not AWS? (Select two)

A. dedicated cloud server

B. hypervisor

C. operating system level

D. application level

E. upstream physical switch

Answer

Amazon AWS tenants are responsible for monitoring of guest operating system and application level security. That includes security updates, maintenance, fixes and appliances that protect tenant data. In addition there are compliance issues and user authentication that tenants must deploy. Monitoring of application level and operating system metrics is the responsibility of tenants. (C,D)

Question 27:

What security authentication is required before configuring or modifying EC2 instances? (Select three)

A. authentication at the operating system level

B. EC2 instance authentication with asymmetric keys

C. authentication at the application level

D. Telnet username and password

E. SSH/RDP session connection

Answer

RSA asymmetric keys include a public key and a private key. The tenant must download and store the private key themselves. In addition there is access to the EC2 instance with SSH (Linux) or Windows (RDP) and authentication at the operating system level. (A,B,E)

Question 28:

What feature is part of Amazon Trusted Advisor?

A. security compliance

B. troubleshooting tool

C. EC2 configuration tool

D. security certificates

Answer

Trusted Advisor is an assessment tool that identifies common security misconfigurations and vulnerabilities. There are suggested best practices as well for improving system performance based on current utilization of EC2 instance for example. (A)

Question 29:

What are two best practices for account management within Amazon AWS?

A. do not use root account for common administrative tasks

B. create a single AWS account with multiple IAM users that have root privilege

C. create multiple AWS accounts with multiple IAM users per AWS account

D. use root account for all administrative tasks

E. create multiple root user accounts for redundancy

Answer

Amazon AWS recommends that tenants only use root account for tasks where it is required. The use of root accounts for common administrative tasks that do not require root privilege is a security issue. Errors such as mistaken delete do not occur with accounts that do not have or require that permission level. The options are typically to create a single AWS account with multiple IAM users that explicitly grant security permissions for various requirements. In addition multiple AWS accounts can be created each with IAM users per account for a granular permissions schema. IAM supports assigning security policies to a group and adding multiple users to the IAM group. That makes it easier to grant access for a single AWS account. (A,C)

Question 30:

What AWS feature is recommended for optimizing data security?

A. Multi-factor authentication

B. username and encrypted password

C. Two-factor authentication

D. SAML

E. Federated LDAP

Answer

Amazon AWS provides a service called Multi-factor authentication (MFA) that is similar to the well-known Two-Factor Authentication. The tenant is prompted for an authentication code after providing the required username and password. It adds some additional credentials to verify users before access to data is granted.

The best strategy is to explicitly assign permissions to an IAM group that allow or prevent specific activities. That would include read-only access to prevent deletion or overwrite. They are common problems in addition to file read access for privacy or granting a user administrative privileges. AWS identity credentials only apply to AWS managed infrastructure (S3 buckets etc.) however they often work in concert with tenant application credentials. (A)

Question 31:

What IAM class enables an EC2 instance to access a file object in an S3 bucket?

A. user

B. root

C. role

D. group

Answer

The solution is an Identity and Access Management (IAM) role that is created by the administrator and assigned read-only permission to access the S3 bucket. The EC2 instance (application) is launched with the role and accesses the file on an S3 bucket. (C)

Question 32:

What are three recommended solutions that provide protection and mitigation from distributed denial of service (DDoS) attacks?

A. security groups

B. CloudWatch

C. encryption

D. WAF

E. data replication

F. Auto-Scaling

Answer

AWS provide static filtering methods available to tenants for inbound and outbound traffic. That includes security groups and Network ACLs assignable to each VPC. In addition there are commercial solutions such as Web Application Firewall that provide packet inspection and malware filtering in front of web servers. CloudWatch can be configured to alert when unusual traffic loads are occurring to respond accordingly and mitigate effects of any attack. (A,B,D)

Question 33:

What are three recommended best practices when configuring Identity and Access Management (IAM) security services?

A. Lock or delete your root access keys when not required

B. IAM groups are not recommended for storage security

C. create an IAM user with administrator privileges

D. share your password and/or access keys with members of your group only

E. delete any AWS account where the access keys are unknown

Answer

Identity and Access Management is used to create and manage AWS user accounts, groups and security permissions for cloud services. The security policies are accessed from the AWS management console. AWS recommends that you do not use your root user credentials to access AWS cloud services.

In addition delete the root user access keys and use it only for intended purposes. That would include modifying support plans, billing and activating various services. The root user has unlimited access to all AWS cloud services associated with an account. It is not possible to assign security permissions that limit root user access.

Create multiple IAM users and groups with granular security permissions based on requirements. For instance create multiple IAM users that require administrator level access privileges. Create an administrator group, attach the AWS *AdministratorAccess* managed policy and assign them to the group. That enables them to create multiple IAM users and define individual security access for a variety of cloud services.

Amazon AWS has a best practice called - Grant Least Privilege, that recommends initially assigning the minimum security permissions to an IAM user that permits doing the requested work. Increase security access for the user based on requirements and functionality. The user access levels include List, Read, Write and Permissions. Granting the permissions access level allows the user to perform security administrator tasks for the cloud service. That could include changing security permission for access to an S3 bucket. (A,C,E)

Question 34:

What two features create security zones between EC2 instances within a VPC?

A. security groups

B. Virtual Security Gateway

C. network ACL

D. WAF

Answer

Migrating applications to the cloud require the same complex granular security policies defined at the enterprise data center. The Cisco Virtual Security Gateway (VSG) is a Layer 2 distributed firewall for east-west traffic between EC2 instances. It is a standalone virtual appliance that is deployed as an EC2 instance.

The VSG works in concert with the Cisco Nexus 1000V switch to enforce logical security zones. There are security policies that must be configured between public and private server zones. There are AWS security groups available as well that support inbound and outbound rules for traffic between EC2 instances. (A,B)

Question 35:

What AWS service provides vulnerability assessment services to tenants within the cloud?

A. Amazon WAF

B. Amazon Inspector

C. Amazon Cloud Logic

D. Amazon Trusted Advisor

Answer

Amazon Inspector is a security assessment service available from AWS that scans infrastructure for security vulnerabilities and makes recommendations. That is based on known current vulnerabilities with applications for example. Trusted Advisor is used for cost optimization in addition to advising tenants on best practices for performance optimization and security. (B)

Question 36:

What are two primary differences between AD Connector and Simple AD for cloud directory services?

A. Simple AD requires an on-premises ADS directory

B. Simple AD is fully managed and setup in minutes

C. AD Connector requires an on-premises ADS directory

D. Simple AD is more scalable than AD Connector

E. Simple AD provides enhanced integration with IAM

Answer

AD connector is a proxy service that enables sign-on to Amazon WorkSpaces, WorkDocs and WorkMail. In addition tenants can join Windows-based instances to an ADS domain and map ADS identities to IAM roles for federated sign-on to AWS management console. Simple AD is an ADS managed service that is limited in scalability and designed for smaller ADS deployments within the cloud. (B,C)

Database Services

Question 1:

How is load balancing enabled for multiple tasks to the same container instance?

A. path-based routing

B. reverse proxy

C. NAT

D. dynamic port mapping

E. dynamic listeners

Answer

The support for Layer 7 load balancing make Application Load Balancer (ALB) well suited to ECS container services. ALB can load balance multiple requests to a single or multiple containers that are each comprised of multiple applications. The traditional load balancer HTTP listener rules are based on content with 1:1 application port mapping. Each application is assigned an application port for such routing purposes.

AWS now supports assigning unused ports for requests with dynamic port mapping. That allows tenants to run multiple copies of the same task on the same container host (EC2 instance). AWS deploys cluster management to create clusters and assigns EC2 instances for launching containers based on tenant requirements. (D)

Question 2:

What encryption support is available for tenants that are deploying AWS DynamoDB?

A. server-side encryption

B. client-side encryption

C. client-side and server-side encryption

D. encryption not supported

E. block level encryption

Answer

There is only client-side encryption (Java) available to tenants that are using DynamoDB database services. The tenant obtains an encryption key from AWS KMS service for that purpose. All data is encrypted while it is in-transit and at rest on DynamoDB. AWS KMS is used to decrypt keys when requests are made from tenants. (B)

Question 3:

What are three primary reasons for deploying ElastiCache?

A. data security

B. managed service

C. replication with Redis

D. durability

E. low latency

Answer

ElastiCache is a managed service that offloads the deployment and maintenance of a multi-purpose elastic scale caching environment from tenants. The cache stores a key-value pair that is much faster than running queries directly on a database. In addition previous results of complex queries are cached for fast access instead of repeating query. There is high performance response time and no charge for unnecessary queries making it cost effective.

Tenants are recommended to cache static content that is frequently accessed for optimized advantages. In addition determine the tolerance for staleness and what affect that has on your application ecosystem. Any content that changes often and not accessed as much is outdated faster and not suitable for caching. ElastiCache architecture does not provide the same level of durability as S3 for example however there is lower latency for data access. Redis caching engine supports replication with clusters for fault tolerance. (B,C,E)

Question 4:

What service does not support session data persistence store to enable web-based stateful applications?

A. RDS

B. Memcached

C. DynamoDB

D. Redis

E. RedShift

Answer

Amazon AWS Elasticache clusters are comprised of multiple Elasticache nodes running instances of Memcached or Redis caching engine. Each cluster must run the same caching engine on node instances within ElastiCache. There is no support for using Memcached as persistence session store to enable stateful applications. It is a caching solutions only where the associated database would store stateful web session data for persistence. There is support however with Redis caching engine for that purpose. (B)

Question 5:

How does Memcached implement horizontal scaling?

A. Auto-Scaling

B. database store

C. partitioning

D. EC2 instances

E. S3 bucket

Answer

Memcached architecture partitions tenant data across multiple nodes that create a cluster for horizontal scaling. The default support is from 1 to 20 nodes that can be added or removed. Scaling any Memcached cluster up or down requires the tenant to create a new cluster. (C)

Question 6:

What two options are available for tenants to access ElastiCache?

A. VPC peering link

B. EC2 instances

C. EFS mount

D. cross-region VPC

Answer

ElastiCache is a web service that provides a distributed, redundant and scalable cache for frequently accessed data. It is accessed through EC2 instances from the VPC where the ElastiCache instance was launched. ElastiCache instance can be accessed from an EC2 instance in a VPC connected across a VPC peering link as well. Each tenant application is configured with an endpoint for connecting to ElastiCache. Each node/cluster is assigned a unique address that creates an endpoint used for connecting applications to caching services. (A,B)

Figure 9 ElastiCache Operation

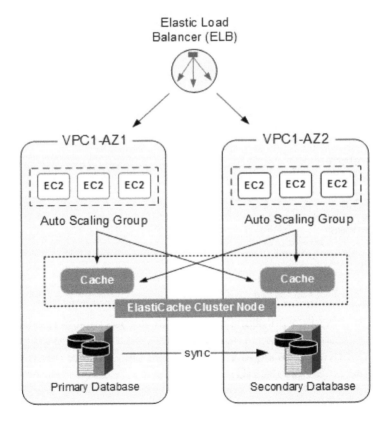

Question 7:

What two statements correctly describe in-transit encryption support on ElastiCache platform ?

A. not supported for ElastiCache platform

B. supported on Redis replication group

C. encrypts cached data at rest

D. not supported on Memcached cluster

E. IPsec must be enabled first

Answer

In-transit encryption is supported only for Redis replication groups running in an Amazon VPC. You can enable in-transit encryption on a replication group only when creating the replication group. In-transit encryption encrypts data when it is forwarded between replication group and application. In addition TLS must be the encryption protocol deployed on the database. AWS ElastiCache for Redis supports at-rest encryption when it is enabled on a replication group. The data is encrypted for all disk operations. (B,D)

Question 8:

What Amazon AWS platform is designed for complex analytics of a variety of large data sets based on custom code. The applications include machine learning and data transformation?

A. EC2

B. Beanstalk

C. CloudFormation

D. Redshift

E. EMR

Answer

EMR enable tenants to run analytics on large data sets based on custom code for a variety of complex applications. Redshift by contrast is used for real-time and offline SQL queries only and business intelligence analytical reporting tools.

RedShift data is structured while EMR can run analytics on unstructured data. There is additional cost associated with EMR so tenants would typically not run SQL queries with it for example. (E)

Question 9:

What are two primary advantages of DynamoDB?

A. SQL support

B. managed service

C. performance

D. CloudFront integration

Answer

DynamoDB is a fully managed database service that provides high throughput and low latency performance. In addition there is auto-replication across three Availability Zones. (B,C)

Question 10:

What two fault tolerant features are supported with Amazon RDS?

A. copy snapshot to a different region

B. create read replica to a different region

C. copy unencrypted read-replica only

D. copy read/write replica and snapshot

Answer

Amazon AWS supports copying EBS Snapshots between different regions. In addition tenants can create read replicas of an encrypted database to a different region. Any encrypted data remains encrypted while in transit as well.

The source database is encrypted at rest and while in transit for read replications to slave databases within the cloud. Any read replication requires selecting a target region and encryption key for target region. You can use your own key or default key generated by KVM in the target region.

The source database sends only read-only replica updates after the initial synchronization to slave database/s has occurred. This is a key aspect of deploying fault tolerant systems with minimal to no downtime. There is currently support for up to five in-region and cross-region replicas supported per API call. In addition Amazon permits a maximum of 40 RDS database instances. (A,B)

Question 11:

What managed services are included with Amazon RDS? (select four)

A. assign network capacity to database instances

B. install database software

C. perform regular backups

D. data replication across multiple availability zones

E. data replication across single availability zone only

F. configure database

G. performance tuning

Answer

Amazon RDS is designed to provide database ready services to tenants with minimal setup. The tenant is responsible for any application level configuration and AWS security through IAM policies. Amazon installs instances, assigns capacity, performs backups and replicates data automatically to multiple Availability Zones.

Amazon AWS Database Migration Service (DMS) enables tenants to easily migrate an on-premises SQL database to Amazon AWS RDS managed service. The service is initiated from Amazon DMS console where source and destination endpoints are configured to replicate database to the cloud. There are additional settings as well that determine how the database is replicated including transformation rules, monitoring checks and logging. Identity and Access Management (IAM) security policies are configured by tenants based on their requirements. It is typically similar permissions and roles they have when the database was originally on-premises at the enterprise data center. (A,B,C,D)

Question 12:

What two configuration features are required to create a private database instance?

A. security group

B. network ACL

C. CloudWatch

D. Elastic IP (EIP)

E. Nondefault VPC

F. DNS

Answer

The database instance includes all compute and storage attributes assigned to a database/s. It defines all components and settings of a full-fledged database environment. Amazon AWS tenants often have multiple database instances for high availability and failover purposes assigned to a private subnet. The tenant must assign a security group to a database instance. In addition enable DNS hostname and DNS resolution attributes to resolve DNS requests. (A,F)

Question 13:

What storage type is recommended for an online transaction processing (OLTP) application deployed to Multi-AZ RDS with significant workloads?

A. General Purpose SSD

B. Magnetic

C. EBS volumes

D. Provisioned IOPS

Answer

The three storage types available with Amazon RDS include General Purpose (SSD), Provisioned IOPS and Magnetic. Tenants can select a storage type and database instance type for vertical scaling when initiating Amazon RDS services for an application. The storage type recommended for transaction processing applications with large I/O intensive workloads is Provisioned IOPS.

The IOPS rate and storage space allocation is selected from a range available by the tenant when the database instance is created. In addition you can allocate additional storage and/or convert to a different storage type at any time.

The database instance type used with database instances specifies capacity with number of IOPS and network throughput (Mbps). Amazon recommends a subset of instance types (M4,M3,R4,R3,M2) that are optimized for IOPS storage when the database is using Provisioned IOPS storage type. General Purpose (SSD) storage type is typically used for small to medium sized databases with moderate workloads and IOPS throughput requirements. (D)

Question 14:

What features are supported with Amazon RDS? (Select three)

A. horizontal scaling with multiple read replicas

B. elastic load balancing RDS read replicas

C. replicate read replicas cross-region

D. automatic failover to master database instance

E. application load balancer (ALB)

Answer

Amazon RDS enables horizontal scaling with read replicas that allow you to elastically scale out as database workloads increase. Multiple read requests are routed (split) among read replicas to improve throughput and lower latency for average and peak traffic events. Read replicas are read-only copies that are synchronized with a source (master) database instance. There is support as well for locating read replicas in a different AWS Region closer to customers or employees for minimizing latency.

Any read replica can be promoted to a master for faster recovery in the event of a disaster. It is not an automatic failover however and not the optimal solution for fault tolerance that is available with Multi-AZ standby replica. The native transparent load balancing is used to forward queries between all database instances that are assigned a unique DNS hostname making it an endpoint. Currently there is no support for deploying ELB with Amazon RDS. The recommended solution for advanced load balancing is AWS Application Load Balancer or HAProxy. (A,C,E)

Question 15:

What are three advantages of standby replica in a Multi-AZ RDS deployment?

A. fault tolerance

B. eliminate I/O freezes

C. horizontal scaling

D. vertical scaling

E. data redundancy

Answer

AWS RDS is a managed relational database service that supports Multi-AZ deployment to optimize fault tolerance and scaling. The fault tolerance is a standby replica that automatically provisions and maintains a synchronous standby replica in a different Availability Zone. RDS primary database instance is synchronously replicated across Availability Zones to a standby replica.

There is automatic failure detection and failover to the standby replica for disaster recovery purposes. The advantages are fault tolerance, data redundancy and eliminating I/O freezes to the hard drive subsystem. It makes system maintenance much easier as well when a standby replica is available during software maintenance windows. (A,B,E)

Question 16:

What consistency model is the default used by DynamoDB?

A. strongly consistent

B. eventually consistent

C. no default model

D. casual consistency

E. sequential consistency

Answer

The default consistency model used by DynamoDB is eventually consistent. It provides higher throughput and lower latency however stale reads (not current) are sometimes returned. Tenants can select strongly consistent model that provides the most updated data that is not stale. (B)

Question 17:

What does RDS use for database and log storage?

A. EBS

B. S3

C. instance store

D. local store

E. SSD

Answer

Amazon RDS use Amazon Elastic Block Store (EBS) volumes for database and log storage. In addition tenants can increase allocated storage available with multiple striped EBS volumes. (A)

Question 18:

What statements correctly describe support for Microsoft SQL Server within Amazon VPC? (Select three)

A. read/write replica

B. read replica only

C. vertical scaling

D. native load balancing

E. EBS storage only

F. S3 storage only

Answer

RDS managed service support Microsoft SQL Server database mirroring and vertical scaling. Microsoft SQL Server primary database mirrors real-time data to a standby replication server for fault tolerance. Database requests are redirected to the standby server for failover only when the primary is not available. As a result only the warm standby service is available with SQL server for disaster recovery.

Amazon supports backup/restore of SQL server database instances to S3 storage as well. RDS provides vertical scaling of SQL database instances for increasing capacity. Tenants can increase allocated storage to the database instance and/or assign a larger instance type. (B,C,D)

Question 19:

Select two features available with Amazon RDS for MySQL?

A. Auto-Scaling

B. read requests to standby replicas

C. real-time database replication

D. active read requests only

Answer

There is support for real-time database replication with RDS for MySQL database instances and Multi-AZ failover. The master and standby replicas are assigned to different Availability Zones. The primary database server replicates data in real time to standby replicas. That allows the tenant to send read requests to the primary and replica database instances. That feature is not available with Microsoft SQL Server for RDS. In addition RDS manages failover to the replica during an outage. Database requests are redirected to the standby replica when the primary database is not available. (B,C)

Question 20:

What are two characteristics of Amazon RDS?

A. database managed service

B. NoSQL queries

C. native load balancer

D. database write replicas

E. automatic failover of read replica

Answer

Amazon RDS is a database managed service from Amazon that supports multiple database servers. Amazon manages the tenant database as a managed service. Amazon RDS enables horizontal scaling with read replicas that allow you to elastically scale out as database workloads increase. Multiple read requests are routed (split) among read replicas to improve throughput and lower latency for average and peak traffic events. Read replicas are read-only copies that are synchronized with a source (master) database instance. There is support as well for locating read replicas in a different AWS Region closer to customers or employees for minimizing latency. Any read replica can be promoted to a master for faster recovery in the event of a disaster. It is not an automatic failover however and not the optimal solution for fault tolerance that is available with Multi-AZ standby replica.

The native transparent load balancing is used to forward queries between all database instances that are assigned a unique DNS hostname making it an endpoint. Currently there is no support for deploying ELB with Amazon RDS. The recommended solution for advanced load balancing is AWS Application Load Balancer or HAProxy. The database servers are assigned to instance types that are supported with Amazon RDS. The data at rest is encrypted with AES256 cipher encryption. Amazon RDS creates an SSL certificate on the database instance automatically when it is created. These certificates are signed by a certificate authority. The SSL certificate includes the DB instance endpoint as the Common Name for SSL certificate to prevent spoofing attacks. (A,C)

Question 21:

What caching engines are supported with Amazon ElastiCache? (Select two)

A. HAProxy

B. Route 53

C. RedShift

D. Redis

E. Memcached

F. CloudFront

Answer

Amazon ElastiCache service supports fast caching to database servers. ElastiCache allows the tenant to store often accessed data from multiple databases. The strategy offloads processing from database servers to optimize data access time. Network latency is decreased and response time minimized. AWS supports the popular Memcached and Redis caching engines. (D,E)

Question 22:

What are three primary characteristics of DynamoDB?

A. less scalable than RDS

B. static content

C. store metadata for S3 objects

D. replication to three Availability Zones

E. high read/write throughput

Answer

DynamoDB is a managed database service that is deployed for applications that require fast concurrent read/write lookups for smaller records. There is virtually unlimited scalability with capacity added automatically based on throughput requirements. The automatic partitioning model seamlessly distributes the data across multiple partitions for speed and storage capacity. It is often used for store and retrieve of frequently accessed records.

The use cases include storing metadata for S3 objects that enable complex index and searches. In addition with the streams feature enable store and retrieve for web page clickstreams and IoT sensor data. The DynamoDB applications as mentioned are based on dynamic data that requires increased storage over time. Amazon auto-replicates tables to three Availability Zones within a region by default for fault tolerance. (C,D,E)

Question 23:

What are three examples of using Lambda functions to move data between AWS services?

A. read data directly from DynamoDB streams to RDS

B. read data from Kinesis stream and write data to DynamoDB

C. read data from DynamoDB stream to Firehose and write to S3

D. read data from S3 and write metadata to DynamoDB

E. read data from Kinesis Firehose to Kinesis data stream

Answer

Lambda functions are increasingly used to enable complex application operations and data migration between multiple AWS services. Each service has particular features that Lambda functions leverage to enable various store-transform-analyze processes for big data. The Lambda functions can read data from multiple sources including Kinesis streams, DynamoDB and S3. In addition Lambda can write to DynamoDB and S3 storage.

AWS Firehose delivery stream now supports data write to RedShift or S3. The data written from Firehose or DynamoDB to RedShift for instance is typically used for real-time analysis of data. Application data from IoT sensors can be streamed through Kinesis data streams as well and saved to DynamoDB for store and retrieval purposes. There is no current support for directly moving DynamoDB streams to RDS. They are separate database platforms with different data structures. In addition data from Kinesis Firehose originates from Kinesis data streams. (B,C,D)

Question 24:

You have enabled Amazon RDS database services in VPC1 for an application with public web servers in VPC2. How do you connect the web servers to the RDS database instance so they can communicate considering the VPC's are in different regions?

A. VPC endpoints

B. VPN gateway

C. path-based routing

D. publicly accessible database

E. VPC peering

Answer

Any traffic sent between EC2 instances and/or AWS services in different regions (cross-region) must traverse the internet. Each VPC must have an Internet gateway in a public subnet and a default route in the custom route table to the Internet gateway.

EC2 instances for the web servers and the RDS database instance are assigned to a public subnet associated to a custom route table within each VPC. In addition, EC2 instances and database instance/s are assigned Elastic IP (EIP) addresses for internet access. It is preferable to use EIP instead of public IPv4 addresses for persistence. The database instance in VPC1 must allow public access. RDS automatically creates a public subnet for your database instance when selecting VPC option to create new VPC and Publicly Accessible option to Yes. (D)

Question 25:

You have a requirement to create an index to search customer objects stored in S3 buckets. The solution should enable you to create a metadata search index for each object stored to an S3 bucket. Select the most scalable and cost effective solution?

A. RDS, ElastiCache

B. DynamoDB, Lambda

C. RDS, EMR, ALB

D. RedShift

Answer

The easiest and most scalable solution is to use DynamoDB (or Elasticsearch) for storing metadata index. Front end EC2 instances are used as data collectors that forward objects to S3 buckets. Create a Lambda function that is invoked by an S3 bucket event notification when a new object is created. The Lambda function updates DynamoDB table with an index entry for the new object. (B)

Question 26:

What are three advantages of using DynamoDB over S3 for storing IoT sensor data where there are 100,000 datapoint samples sent per minute?

A. S3 must create a single file for each event

B. IoT can write data directly to DynamoDB

C. DynamoDB provides fast read/writes to a structured table for queries

D. DynamoDB is designed for frequent access and fast lookup of small records

E. S3 is designed for frequent access and fast lookup of smaller records

F. IoT can write data directly to S3

Answer

The preferred solution for IoT sensor data is DynamoDB where there are larger datapoint read/writes per minute. Sensors can write directly to DynamoDB tables with a datapoint range from 1 byte to 400 KB. In addition it is designed for frequent access and fast lookup of smaller records. S3 is less structured and creates a single file for each event this is cumbersome. In addition Firehose is typically required for datapoint write to S3. Moving sensor data from DynamoDB to RedShift for analytics is easier as well. Consider for example creating time series tables for sensor data based on time stamps. (B,C,D)

Question 27:

Your company is a provider of online gaming that customers access with various network access devices including mobile phones. What is a data warehousing solutions for large amounts of information on player behavior, statistics and events for analysis using SQL tools?

A. RedShift

B. DynamoDB

C. RDS

D. DynamoDB

E. Elasticsearch

Answer

RedShift is well suited for Petabyte amounts of data warehousing to run SQL analytical tools. Online gaming is an application that generates TB+ amounts of data that can be analyzed and used for adding new features and optimize marketing strategies. (A)

Question 28:

What two statements are correct when comparing Elasticsearch and RedShift as analytical tools?

A. Elasticsearch is a text search engine and document indexing tool

B. RedShift supports complex SQL-based queries with Petabyte sized data store

C. Elasticsearch supports SQL queries

D. RedShift provides only basic analytical services

E. Elasticsearch does not support JSON data type

Answer

Elasticsearch is a text search engine and document indexing tool that provides basic analytical features. RedShift is a data warehouse that supports complex SQL-based queries and BI reporting tools with Petabyte sized data store. (A,B)

Question 29:

What happens when read or write requests exceed capacity units (throughput capacity) for a DynamoDB table or index? (Select two)

A. DynamoDB automatically increases read/write units

B. DynamoDB can throttle requests so that requests are not exceeded

C. HTTP 400 code is returned (Bad Request)

D. HTTP 500 code is returned (Server Error)

E. DynamoDB automatically increases read/write units if provisioned throughput is enabled

Answer

DynamoDB will automatically throttle read or write requests when they exceed current throughput configured settings. That includes requests to a table or an index. The purpose of throttling is to prevent an application from consuming too many capacity units. AWS returns an HTTP 400 code (Bad Request) when throttling is initiated. (B,C)

Question 30:

What read consistency method provides lower latency for *GetItem* requests?

A. strongly persistent

B. eventually consistent

C. strongly consistent

D. write consistent

Answer

DynamoDB provides a low latency storage service with different storage classes. There is write replication of data across tables in three Availability Zones for durability and fault tolerance. DynamoDB returns an HTTP 200 code to your application when all copies of the data are updated to all zones. The default setting is eventually consistent reads where data that was previously written is available faster however the read could include some stale data. There is lower latency with eventually consistent reads as a result. The data is eventually consistent across all storage locations typically within one second or less. (B)

Question 31:

You must specify strongly consistent read and write capacity for your DynamoDB database. You have determined read capacity of 128 Kbps and write capacity of 25 Kbps is required for your application. What is the read and write capacity units required for DynamoDB table?

A. 32 read units, 25 write units

B. 1 read unit, 1 write unit

C. 16 read units, 2.5 write units

D. 64 read units, 10 write units

Answer

DynamoDB specifies one read capacity unit as a single read per second for an item (record) up to 4 KB in size. In addition one write capacity unit as a single write per second for an item of up to 1 KB in size. The read capacity of 128 Kbps would require 32 read units (128 kbps = 4 KB x 32 units). The write capacity of 25 Kbps would require 25 write units (25 Kbps = 1 KB x 25 units). (A)

Question 32:

What DynamoDB capacity management technique is based on the tenant specifying an upper and lower range for read/write capacity units?

A. demand

B. provisioned throughput

C. reserved capacity

D. auto scaling

Answer

DynamoDB supports Auto-Scaling that allows tenants to configure a range of capacity units with a maximum value. That enables capacity units to be increased temporarily during periods of peak traffic and prevent throttling. DynamoDB publishes capacity metrics to CloudWatch and any exceeded event triggers a CloudWatch alarm and an SNS notification. The alarm invokes Auto Scaling feature within DynamoDB to increase or decrease capacity units. (D)

Question 33:

What is the maximum volume size of a MySQL RDS database?

A. 6 TB

B. 3 TB

C. 16 TB

D. unlimited

Answer

AWS RDS is a database managed service that supports MySQL, SQL Server and Oracle database servers for tenants. The customizable features for the tenant are limited as a result. Amazon RDS recently increased maximum database storage size up to 16 TB when using Provisioned IOPS and General Purpose (SSD) storage. Standard redundancy features include multiple availability zones (Multi-AZ) and read replication for scalability.

AWS managed services including Amazon RDS for Oracle and SQL Server support TDE style encryption. There is a backup service with the *Snapshot Copy* feature and security permissions assigned to the tenant. RDS creates a database instance with multiple database tables with assigned processing and volume disk size. The advantage of larger database size and higher IOPS is higher workloads on a single Amazon RDS instance without distributing (shard) the data across multiple instances. (C)

Question 34:

What is the maximum size of a DynamoDB record (item)?

A. 400 KB

B. 64 KB

C. 1 KB

D. 10 KB

Answer

The maximum size of an item (record) that can be stored in a DynamoDB table is 400 KB. Tenants can store large attributes as an S3 object for items that exceed the maximum 400 KB limit. There is support for a variety of data types including JSON documents, web session state and blobs. (A)

Fault Tolerant Systems

Question 1:

What two features correctly describe an Application Load Balancer (ALB)?

A. dynamic port mapping

B. SSL listener

C. layer 7 load balancer

D. backend server authentication

E. multi-region forwarding

Answer

AWS Elastic Load Balancer distributes traffic within a single VPC to provide scalability and redundancy for applications. Each application is often comprised of multiple tiers located in different Availability Zones. As a result ELB can easily load balance traffic among multiple Availability Zones. The ELB service defines Classic, Application and Network load balancers.

Application Load Balancer (ALB) is a managed service that can load balance up to ten different applications per ALB. The ALB is scaled automatically as traffic workload increases. It terminates incoming connections, examines the HTTP header and forwards packets based on a rule set. It acts as a proxy where packet rewrite occurs on the ALB. HTTP header contains an *X-forwarded-for* field with the client IP address. In addition Application Load Balancer supports path-based routing and dynamic port mapping. The purpose of dynamic port mapping is to route multiple tasks per service to a single container instance. (A,C)

Question 2:

What enables load balancing between multiple applications per load balancer?

A. listeners

B. sticky sessions

C. path-based routing

D. backend server authentication

Answer

Amazon AWS provides path-based routing feature with Application Load Balancer (ALB). The purpose is to enable load balancing among multiple applications with a single ALB. The inbound request is routed to an individual application (and member EC2 instance) based on the URL matching a listener rule. The URL refers to a domain and web page used for distinguishing applications and member EC2 instances. (C)

Question 3:

What three features are characteristic of Classic Load Balancers?

A. dynamic port mapping

B. path-based routing

C. SSL listener

D. backend server authentication

E. ECS

F. Layer 4 based load balancer

Answer

Classic Load Balancer is Layer 4 connection-oriented where incoming requests are equally distributed across multiple instances for a single application only. There is support for TCP and SSL listeners not available with an Application Load Balancer. Amazon AWS recommends that tenants deploy the same number of EC2 instances per load balancing group in each Availability Zone. In addition enable cross-zone load balancing for optimized results.

Application and Classic Load Balancers have listeners that define the protocol and port, where the load balancer listens for incoming connections. Each load balancer must have at least one listener with support for ten listeners. Routing rules for path-based routing are defined on listeners along with targets and target groups. Classic Load Balancers support HTTP, HTTPS, TCP and SSL protocols from clients while Application Load Balancers only HTTP and HTTPS. (C,D,F)

Question 4:

What security feature is only available with Classic Load Balancer?

A. IAM role

B. SAML

C. back-end server authentication

D. security groups

E. LDAP

Answer

EC2 instances are authenticated to Classic Load Balancer with a public key. The load balancer only communicates with an EC2 instance when the public keys match. In addition SSL and security certificates are supported for in-transit data security. (C)

Question 5:

What is a primary difference between Classic and Network Load Balancer?

A. IP address target

B. Auto-Scaling

C. protocol target

D. cross-zone load balancing

E. listener

Answer

Network Load Balancers support IP address targets including outside of the VPC. In addition there is support for containers and dynamic port mapping. In addition there is additional scalability to millions of requests per second. (A)

Question 6:

What are the first two conditions used by Amazon AWS default termination policy for Multi-AZ architecture?

A. unprotected instance with oldest launch configuration

B. Availability Zone (AZ) with the most instances

C. at least one instance that is not protected from scale in

D. unprotected instance closest to the next billing hour

E. random selection of any unprotected instance

Answer

The default termination policy is designed to ensure instances are distributed evenly across multiple Availability Zones. When using the default termination policy, Auto Scaling selects an instance to terminate based on two conditions initially. The Availability Zone (AZ) with the most instances and where at least one instance is not protected from scale in. Where there is a tie, it is an unprotected instance with oldest launch configuration terminated. (B,C)

Question 7:

What feature is used for horizontal scaling of consumers to process data records from a Kinesis data stream?

A. vertical scaling shards

B. Auto-Scaling

C. Lambda

D. Elastic Load Balancer

Answer

Consumers are EC2 instances that process (include transform) data records and forward them to storage, database or Kinesis firehose platform for analysis. Consider for example the large scale amount of data that results from millions of remote wireless sensors sending real-time data to an application. There is virtually unlimited capacity with Auto-Scaling of EC2 instances for real-time processing particularly when peak traffic loads occur. (B)

Question 8:

What DNS records can be used for pointing a zone apex to an Elastic Load Balancer or CloudFront distribution? (Select two)

A. Alias

B. CNAME

C. MX

D. A

E. Name Server

Answer

Based on standard DNS specifications, all (A) records resolve a hostname to an IP address. In addition the Alias record is a DNS extension that resolves a hostname to another hostname. The Alias record type is used specifically to alias the root domain (zone apex).

For example a zone apex is domain name cisconetsolutions.com (instead of subdomain www.cisconetsolutions.com). Tenants would use Alias Records within AWS to map a tenant zone apex in a hosted zone to either an ELB, CloudFront distribution, Beanstalk or S3 bucket of a tenant. An example is mapping tenant zone apex (yourwebapp.com) to another target such as Elastic Load Balancer DNS name (elb2345.elb.amazonaws.com). The 'A' record for the ELB is then used to resolve the hostname to IP address of the ELB. The advantage of Alias records is faster update of DNS records when an IP address changes within the cloud. The hostnames often do not change when assigned to services. In addition it is easier for tenants and customers to use a custom zone apex instead of a complex lengthy Elastic Load Balancer DNS name.

CNAME is used to resolve a hostname to another hostname similar to an Alias. CNAME is typically used for subdomains where www.yourwebapp.com for instance would resolve (point) to amazon.elb.aws.amazon.com (DNS name of ELB). The DNS 'A' record is then used to resolve amazon.elb.aws.amazon.com to its IP address. The CNAME cannot be used to create a record for your zone apex (root domain). The tenant zone file includes DNS resource records (A, Alias, CNAME, MX, NS etc.) used by AWS Route 53 for resolving hostnames to IP addresses for servers and AWS services. Each tenant can manage configuration of DNS Route 53 services to enable internet access for applications, global load balancing and fault tolerant systems. The following describes DNS resolution with different record types when there is a request for a web page. (A,D)

Example DNS Record Lookups:

Client makes request for a web page → DNS Route 53

A Record → amazon.elb.aws.amazon.com = 198.200.1.1

CNAME Record = www.yourwebapp.com = amazon.elb.aws.amazon.com →
    A Record → amazon.elb.aws.amazon.com = 198.200.1.1

ALIAS Record = yourwebapp.com = amazon.elb.aws.amazon.com →
    A Record → amazon.elb.aws.amazon.com = 198.200.1.1

Question 9:

What services are primarily provided by DNS Route 53? (Select three)

A. load balancing web servers within a private subnet

B. resolve hostnames and IP addresses

C. load balancing web servers within a public subnet

D. load balancing data replication requests between ECS containers

E. resolve queries and route internet traffic to AWS resources

F. automated health checks to EC2 instances

Answer

Route 53 is a scalable DNS service that enables resolving queries from internet sources to CloudFront, Elastic Beanstalk, ELB and S3. There is support most resource record types such as MX (mail), A (IP address), canonical name (CNAME) and Name Server (NS). In addition there is support for adding your own domain names and load balancing between primary and failover locations for fault tolerance.

Any global load balancing service basically manages DNS records to affect where packets are forwarded. There is support for a variety of routing policies based on tenant requirements. DNS Route 53 is the service that load balances traffic to individual Elastic Load Balancers. (B,E,F)

Figure 10 DNS Route 53

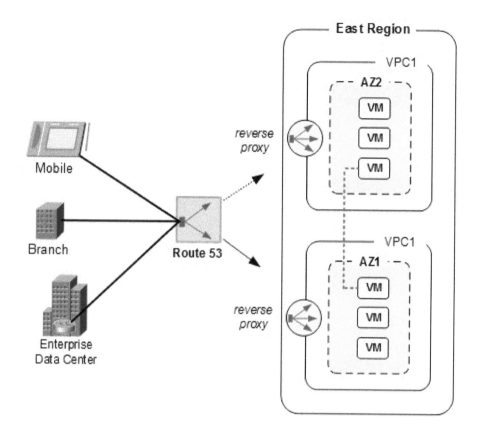

Question 10:

What are two features that correctly describe Availability Zone (AZ) architecture?

A. multiple regions per AZ

B. interconnected with private WAN links

C. multiple AZ per region

D. interconnected with public WAN links

E. data auto-replicated between zones in different regions

F. Direct Connect supports Layer 2 connectivity to region

Answer

Amazon AWS global architecture is comprised of multiple regions with multiple data centers called Availability Zones (AZ) inter-connected within that region. There are high speed links as well that interconnect each region. The private redundant links interconnecting Availability Zones are used to route traffic within the AWS cloud. Internet Gateways are deployed for public connectivity including enterprise on-premises. (B,C)

Question 11:

How is Route 53 configured for Warm Standby fault tolerance? (Select two)

A. automated health checks

B. path-based routing

C. failover records

D. Alias records

Answer

You can create an active/passive failover configuration by using failover records. You create a primary and a secondary failover record that have the same name and type, and you associate a health check with each. The primary and secondary failover records can refer to anything from an Amazon S3 bucket that is configured as a website to a complex tree of records. When all of the resources that are referenced by the primary failover record are unhealthy, Amazon Route 53 automatically begins responding to queries by using the resources that are referenced by the secondary failover record. (A,C)

Question 12:

How is DNS Route 53 configured for Multi-Site fault tolerance? (Select two)

A. IP address

B. weighted records (non-zero)

C. health checks

D. Alias records

E. zero weighted records

Answer

The tenant adds health checks to all of the records in a group of weighted records. In addition there are nonzero weights assigned to all of the records for creating Multi-Site active/active failover. DNS Route 53 cycles through each DNS record based on weight when a record fails health check. The healthy record is then used for responding to the DNS query with an IP address. Health checks are defined by an endpoint, protocol (HTTP, HTTPS,TCP), IP address and port to use for an instance. (B,C)

Question 13:

What is an Availability Zone?

A. data center

B. multiple VPCs

C. multiple regions

D. single region

E. multiple EC2 server instances

Answer

AWS global infrastructure is segmented into regions with multiple availability zones. Each availability zone within a region is a separate data center. The availability zones enable database replication to separate data centers for high availability and disaster recovery. That optimizes redundancy and scalability for applications. Availability zones enable Geo-redundancy for applications and data. That maximizes application uptime and protects data. (A)

Question 14:

How are DNS records managed with Amazon AWS to enable high availability?

A. Auto-Scaling

B. server health checks

C. reverse proxy

D. elastic load balancing

Answer

Amazon DNS Route 53 service manages DNS tables and redirects sessions to available EC2 instances and availability zones. The tenant configures weighting for load balancing across multiple availability zones. Route 53 manages DNS tables and provides dynamic updates to DNS records with reverse proxy feature. Route 53 DNS weighting can forward a percentage of tenant traffic to the VPC and some to a failover data center for global load balancing. Packets can be forwarded to multiple availability zones at the same or different regions for Multi-Site failover and recovery. (C)

Question 15:

Distinguish Warm Standby and Multi-Site fault tolerance? (Select two)

A. Multi-Site enables lower RTO and most recent RPO

B. Warm Standby enables lower RTO and most recent RPO

C. Multi-Site provides active/active load balancing

D. Multi-Site provides active/standby load balancing

E. DNS Route 53 is not required for Warm Standby

Answer

RTO is the time it takes after a disruption to restore services to normal based on an operational level agreement (OLA). RPO is defined as the acceptable amount of data loss during the RTO period. Tenants should create fault tolerant systems with redundancy design that is based on RTO/RPO. The following are Amazon AWS fault tolerant systems designs with varying RTO/RPO levels.

1. Backup and Restore is based on data restore from backups that were made with bulk data transfer or a snapshot service to an S3 bucket. The tenant should as a minimum make backups of on-premises and cloud-based volumes. In addition Amazon auto-replicates data within an Availability Zone. It is a common practice for tenants to make EBS snapshots from EC2 instances. The backup and restore has the highest recovery time of all methods. The RPO = last snapshot and RTO = time to manually restore and start EBS volume.

2. Pilot Light method is based on locating the production application on-premises and duplicating minimal core components at AWS that are not active. There is real-time database replication to Amazon cloud across a Direct Connect link.

The result is a lower RTO/RPO than backup method. RPO = minimal, RTO = time to start instances, failover and establish user sessions establish.

3. Warm Standby is similar to Pilot Light however there are operational web and application servers at AWS running minimally and not processing traffic. The advantage is RTO/RPO is further minimized with a faster failover having AWS EC2 instances operational ready. Amazon AWS automates DNS route 53 traffic redirect to AWS data center with health checks or modify DNS records manually. In addition EC2 instances launch along with ELB and Auto-Scaling. There is a lower RTO/RTO than Pilot Light measured in minutes.

4. Multi-site duplicates the production environment from on-premises to Amazon AWS cloud. DNS route 53 route policies are modified to load balance traffic between on-premises and AWS cloud. DNS route 53 is a global load balancer splitting traffic load between multiple location. There is real-time mirroring or data replication from on-premises database to a slave database in the cloud for database synchronization. The database platform determines whether mirroring or replication is recommended or available. Multi-site design has the lowest RTO and RPO where is near to no downtime. (A,C)

Question 16:

What AWS best practice is recommended for creating fault tolerant systems?

A. vertical scaling

B. Elastic IP (EIP)

C. security groups

D. horizontal scaling

E. RedShift

Answer

Vertical scaling adds or decreases capacity available to a single EC2 instance based on the assigned instance type. The tenant would assign a higher instance type to add capacity and lower instance type to decrease capacity. Horizontal scaling adds or decreases capacity available to an auto-scaling group or database. The tenant can add or remove ec2 instances to an auto-scaling group. That would for instance permit additional user session connections per second to public web servers.

In addition adding read replicas to an RDS managed database would increase database capacity through number of transactions per second. The effect of horizontal scaling is to distribute packets across multiple EC2 instances. (D)

Question 17:

What two statements correctly describe versioning for protecting data at rest on S3 buckets?

A. enabled by default

B. creates snapshots

C. overwrites most current file version

D. restores deleted files

E. saves multiple versions of a single file

F. disabled by default

Answer

There are a variety of features that protect data at rest on S3 volumes. Versioning (disable by default) creates a new version of any file that is deleted or modified. That allows tenants to restore a file that was accidentally deleted. In addition to versioning there is encryption, replication and security controls. Assigning object-level and bucket-level permissions in addition to IAM policies prevents users from unauthorized access and deleting files. (D,F)

Question 18:

What two methods are recommended by AWS for protecting EBS data at rest?

A. replication

B. snapshots

C. encryption

D. VPN

Answer

Snapshots are used to restore a point in time state including all data for a tenant. IAM users, groups and roles are assignable to EBS snapshots to specify access and administrative tasks. Encryption of data at rest is recommended based on the fact that cloud is a public shared domain. Replication is done automatically by AWS however it is not as reliable for a data restore solution. (B,C)

Question 19:

You have an Elastic Load Balancer assigned to a VPC with public and private subnets. ELB is configured to load balance traffic to a group of EC2 instances assigned to an Auto-Scaling group. What three statements are correct?

A. Elastic Load Balancer is assigned to a public subnet

B. network ACL is assigned to Elastic Load Balancer

C. security group is assigned to Elastic Load Balancer

D. cross-zone load balancing is not supported

E. Elastic Load Balancer forwards traffic to primary private IP address (eth0 interface) on each instance

Answer

Tenants connect to EC2 instances assigned to an Auto-Scaling group based on DNS name or IP address of the Elastic Load Balancer. The ELB is assigned to a public subnet with a custom route table that has a default route to the Internet gateway. The tenant can either assign an existing security group or create a new security group for the ELB. The security group must permit inbound and outbound traffic based on the listeners configured. Traffic ingress from the internet is forwarded to the primary private IP address (eth0 interface) of each EC2 instance.

There is cross-zone load balancing support as well where the ELB distributes requests to Auto-Scaling groups in different Availability Zones. There is support for load balancing EC2 instances that are assigned to public and/or private subnets. EC2 instances assigned to a private subnet are configured with private IP addressing only. EC2 instances assigned to a public subnet are configured with at least a single private IP address and an EIP or public IPv4 address. (A,C,E)

Deployment

Question 1:

What Amazon AWS service is available for container management?

A. ECS

B. Docker

C. Kinesis

D. Lambda

Answer

Amazon AWS provides EC2 Container Services (ECS) for easier deployment of Docker-based containers to the cloud. Containers are an alternate architecture to virtual machines. The container requires only minimum operating system files shared by multiple applications. Tenants can run multiple container instances on a single or multiple EC2 instances. That makes it easier to run more complex applications with less memory and CPU usage.

The container is abstracted from the underlying operating system as a result making it lighter and portable within the cloud. The advantages of Elastic Container Service is easier deployment and orchestration of tenant containers that are less costly, scalable and redundant. The tenant only has to create the containers and select parameters for deployment to AWS. (A)

Question 2:

What is typically associated with Microservices? (Select two)

A. Application Load Balancer

B. Kinesis

C. RDS

D. DynamoDB

E. ECS

F. EFS

Answer

Microservices architecture decouples a single application into multiple services that are connected through light APIs. The software development and management approach is decentralized where separate teams are assigned to services. The isolation of services creates more stable, fault tolerant and easier to manage applications. It promotes agility where new features can be added faster based on user requirements. In addition any errors or performance problems are isolated to a single service and do not affect other services. Application Load Balancer and ECS are key to enabling Microservices. (A,E)

Question 3:

Where does Amazon retrieve web content when it is not in the nearest CloudFront edge location?

A. secondary location

B. file server

C. EBS

D. S3 bucket

Answer

If the content is already in the edge location with the lowest latency, CloudFront delivers it immediately. If the content is not in that edge location, CloudFront retrieves it from an Amazon S3 bucket or an HTTP server (web server) that you have identified as the source for the definitive version of your content. (D)

Question 4:

What two features of an API Gateway minimize the effects of peak traffic events and minimize latency?

A. load balancing

B. firewalling

C. throttling

D. scaling

E. caching

154

Answer

Most network throughput within any data center occurs at backend database servers and storage. The use of API to configure, launch and manage AWS services is a key aspect of cloud operations. In fact programmability is based on some API calls to physical and virtual-based infrastructure. API Gateway throttles traffic during peak traffic events to backend systems. In addition the output of API calls are cached to prevent redundant request to backend systems. (C,E)

Question 5:

What three characteristics differentiate Lambda from traditional EC2 deployment or containerization?

A. Lambda is based on Kinesis scripts

B. Lambda is serverless

C. tenant has ownership of EC2 instances

D. tenant has no control of EC2 instances

E. Lambda is a code-based service

F. Lambda supports only S3 and Glacier

Answer

Lambda is a new cloud architecture that now enables serverless computing. The cloud is currently based on the virtual machine as a building block. Tenants currently use a static model where an application is bundled into an AMI and assigned an EC2 instance. ECS containerization is a dynamic model where tenants create containers that support operating system virtualization. Amazon AWS manage deployment and orchestration of containers that are scalable and run on any hardware or operating system.

Amazon AWS makes it possible for developers to submit code in a variety of supported platforms to Lambda. All server management, infrastructure provisioning, redundancy and service orchestration is provided by Lambda. In contrast to Beanstalk, tenants cannot access any EC2 instances or other infrastructure components generated by Lambda. It is abstracted so there is no control of AWS infrastructure. It is primarily used for adding functionality to applications and managing any AWS service. As a result it is further redefining how applications can be deployed and managed. (B,D,E)

Question 6:

How is code uploaded to Lambda?

A. Lambda instance

B. Lambda container

C. Lambda entry point

D. Lambda function

E. Lambda AMI

Answer

Tenants can upload code from any approved software platform as a Lambda function. The code written is stateless where any calls to files or hardware exists only for a single request. Each request is a new transaction and any associated stateful data is stored (persistent) on S3, DynamoDB or RDS. (D)

Question 7:

How are Lambda functions triggered?

A. EC2 instance

B. hypervisor

C. Kinesis

D. operating system

E. event source

Answer

Tenants configure AWS services or custom applications as event sources that publish events to automatically trigger or invoke a Lambda function. It is commonly known as event source mapping and defines Lambda operation. There is a subgroup of AWS services called stream services that include Kinesis and DynamoDB for Lambda functions. (E)

Question 8:

What three statements correctly describe standard Lambda operation?

A. Lambda function is allocated 500 MB ephemeral disk space

B. Lambda function is allocated 100 MB EBS storage

C. Lambda stores code in S3

D. Lambda stores code in a Glacier vault

E. Lambda stores code in containers

F. maximum execution time is 300 seconds

Answer

Lambda stores tenant code in an S3 bucket where it is encrypted. Each function is allocated 500 MB of ephemeral (temporary) storage and maximum execution time is limited to 300 seconds. The maximum number of concurrent executions at any one time is 300. The default timeout is 3 seconds however it is configurable to between 1 and 300 seconds. (A,C,F)

Question 9:

What network events are restricted by Lambda? (Select two)

A. only inbound TCP network connections are blocked by AWS Lambda

B. all inbound network connections are blocked by AWS Lambda

C. all inbound and outbound connections are blocked

D. outbound connections support only TCP/IP sockets

E. outbound connections support only SSL sockets

Answer

Lambda blocks all inbound (public internet) network connections and permits only TCP/IP based outbound connections. In addition all ptrace access is denied and TCP port 25 (anti-spam) is blocked. (B,D)

Question 10:

How is versioning supported with Lambda? (Select two)

A. Lambda native support

B. ECS container

C. not supported

D. Aliases

E. replication

F. S3 versioning

Answer

The purpose of versioning is to maintain multiple versions of a function. Each AWS Lambda function has a single, current version of the code. There is native support for versioning of the same function within Lambda service. Tenants can leverage Aliases feature as well that act as a pointer to a function instead of using the assigned Amazon Resource Name (ARN).

The advantage of Aliases is managing software development and updates for production and testing. It is easier to use an Alias and point it to the Lambda function that is most current instead of all configuration updates required on the event source. Any published Lambda function cannot be changed (immutable) and as a result version and file management becomes a key aspect of the Lambda service. (A,D)

Question 11:

What is the difference between Stream-based and AWS Services when enabling Lambda?

A. streams maintains event source mapping in Lambda

B. streams maintains event source mapping in event source

C. streams maintains event source mapping in EC2 instance

D. streams maintains event source mapping in notification

E. streams maintains event source mapping in API

Answer

The primary difference between AWS services and streams-based event sources is where event source mapping is enabled. The event source mapping for AWS services is located at the event source (S3, Glacier, SNS, RDS etc.). The event source mapping for streams-based DynamoDB and Kinesis are maintained in AWS Lambda. It is a pull model where Lambda polls a stream for specific records and invokes a Lambda function when detected. (A)

Question 12:

Select two custom origin servers from the following?

A. S3 bucket

B. S3 object

C. EC2 instance

D. Elastic Load Balancer

E. API gateway

Answer

CloudFront architecture provides web content from edge locations for the sole purpose of minimizing latency and maximizing throughput. As a result page loads are faster for web-based applications and any downloaded media content.

Origin servers reside at AWS where tenants copy original versions of web page content and media files called objects. The origin server for HTTP content is either an S3 bucket or a web server. The web server can run on an EC2 instance or privately managed server. In addition an elastic load balancer is a custom origin as well. Any source that isn't an S3 bucket is referred to as a custom origin. CloudFront distributes media files on demand using the Adobe Media Server RTMP protocol from an S3 bucket (origin server) only. (C,D)

Question 13:

What two attributes are only associated with CloudFront private content?

A. Amazon S3 URL

B. signed cookies

C. web distribution

D. signed URL

E. object

Answer

Any objects distributed from an S3 bucket can be either public or private read-only. Public content is available to anyone that knows the CloudFront URL. The objects set as private are only available when the signed URL or signed cookies are provided to the user. In addition the users must access private content with CloudFront URLs instead of Amazon S3 URLs for security purposes. (B,D)

Question 14:

How are origin servers located within CloudFront (Select two)

A. DNS request

B. distribution list

C. web distribution

D. RTMP protocol

E. DHCP request

F. source mapping

Answer

The tenant must configure CloudFront web distributions that are used by CloudFront to identify origin servers where objects are stored and any logging options. In addition there is a domain name assigned to a new distribution. CloudFront sends the distribution configuration file to all edge locations that are caching content for the tenant. Media files require a web distribution for media player and RTMP distribution for the media files (on demand streaming). (A,C)

Question 15:

Where are HTML files sourced from when they are not cached at a CloudFront edge location?

A. S3 object

B. origin HTTP server

C. S3 bucket

D. nearest edge location

E. RTMP server

F. failover edge location

Answer

The user starts with a requests to a web server or application owned by the AWS tenant. DNS routes the request to the nearest CloudFront edge location where latency is minimized (least number of hops). CloudFront then checks the edge location cache for the required objects that typically comprise a web page.

The web content is downloaded by the user if it is available. CloudFront forwards the request for image files to an Amazon S3 bucket (origin server) when not available at the edge location. In addition any requests for HTML files not at the edge location are forwarded to the origin HTTP (web) server. By default each object is cached in an edge location for 24 hours. After that a new request is required to copy object from origin server to an edge location where it is cached again. (B)

Question 16:

What is the capacity of a single Kinesis shard? (Select two)

A. 2000 PUT records per second

B. 1 MB/sec data input and 2 MB/sec data output

C. 10 MB/sec data input and 10 MB/sec data output

D. 1000 PUT records per second

E. unlimited

Answer

Kinesis data records are composed of a sequence number, partition key and data blob with a maximum payload size of 1 MB. The shard is a grouping of data records that form the basic element of a data stream. In addition tenants must specify the number of shards when defining a data stream. The capacity of a single shard is 1MB/sec data input and 2MB/sec data output that supports 1000 PUT records per second. The tenant can increase the number of shards to increase data stream capacity based on requirements. (B,D)

Question 17:

What Amazon AWS service supports real-time processing of data stream from multiple consumers and replay of records?

A. DynamoDB

B. EMR

C. Kinesis data streams

D. SQS

E. RedShift

Answer

Kinesis data stream starts with a producer that puts real-time data records into a Kinesis data stream. For example consider a web server that is sending log data to a Kinesis stream. The consumer is an EC2 instance that processes the data records in real-time from a Kinesis stream. Records from a stream are available for up to 24 hours by default however extended data retention enables access up to 7 days. The data stream is processed by a single or multiple consumers running on EC2 instances.

The consumers forward data to storage service such as S3 and/or database services such as RedShift or DynamoDB. The support for adding multiple consumers to a Kinesis data stream and record replay distinguishes Kinesis from SQS. Kinesis also synchronously replicates data across three Availability Zones for redundancy. (C)

Question 18:

Your company has asked you to capture and forward a real-time data stream on a massive scale directly to RedShift for analysis with BI tools. What AWS tool is most appropriate that provides the feature set and cost effective?

A. DynamoDB

B. SQS

C. Elastic Map Reduce

D. Kinesis Firehose

E. SNS

F. CloudFront

Answer

The primary purpose of Kinesis Firehose is to capture a Kinesis data stream and forward it to a supported storage platform. The tenant assigns an EC2 instance (consumer) that forwards a Kinesis stream to Kinesis firehose. The tenant can run Business Intelligence tools for analysis purposes on data loaded to RedShift for example.

The scale of data associated with a Kinesis data stream is massive scale. It enables tenants to run analytical tools and derive a lot of reports and associated results. Firehose is essentially an intermediary to RedShift, Elasticsearch and Splunk for delivery and transformation. There is server-side encryption at rest as well for data security. (D)

Question 19:

What feature permits tenants to use a private domain name instead of the domain name that CloudFront assigns to a distribution?

A. Route 53

B. CNAME record

C. MX record

D. RTMP

E. Signed URL

Answer

CNAME is a DNS record type that permits tenants to use a domain name of their own for links to objects instead of using the domain name that CloudFront assigns to distributions. There is support for URL and RTMP distributions along with a wildcard * for defining multiple subdomains. (B)

Question 20:

What Amazon AWS service is available to guarantee the consuming of a unique message only once?

A. Beanstalk

B. SQL

C. Exchange

D. SQS

Answer

SQS is a hosted queuing service to manage messages and track status to confirm delivery. In addition it supports increasing queue size during peak loads and configure delays for groups of messages. There are only some regions that provide all of the available feature set. (D)

Question 21:

What is the fastest and easiest method for migrating an on-premises VMware virtual machine to the AWS cloud?

A. Amazon Marketplace

B. AWS Server Migration Service

C. AWS Storage Gateway

D. EC2 Import/Export

Answer

The on-premises virtual machine is located typically at the enterprise data center. It is created initially using VMware tools that convert a physical server to a VM. Amazon AWS Server Migration Server (SMS) automates and replicates the VM server volume and saves it as an AMI image from the AWS Console. The AMI can be used to launch an EC2 instance (cloud VM) of a server.

164

AMI can be used to launch multiple EC2 instances such as web servers as well based on auto-scaling for increased compute capacity. An application such as Oracle has multiple Amazon Machine Images (AMI) based on the number of servers required. There is currently no support for converting non-VMware virtual machines using SMS. (B)

Question 22:

Select the stateless protocol from the following?

A. FTP

B. SMTP

C. TCP

D. HTTP

E. SSH

Answer

Stateless applications do not save any session information when a transaction ends. An example of a stateless protocol is HTTP. The stateless application sends a group of requests to a web server where the session data (not the application data) is deleted from cache when the browser starts a new connection. Stateful applications cache session data for clients that is used for multiple transactions during the course of a session for fault tolerance.

The Amazon AWS cloud environment is comprised of multiple instances and redundancy. The tenant can deploy a stateless web-based application and leverage databases such as RDS that can be used to save session information. The ELB would redirect a user session to an available web server for instance when there is a web server failure from an Auto-Scaling group. The web server would query the associated database and retrieve session information. That enables stateful behavior with the associated advantages of elasticity and fault tolerance particularly where ElastiCache is deployed for caching application and session state data. (D)

Question 23:

What are three valid endpoints for an API gateway?

A. RESTful API

B. Lambda function

C. AWS service

D. web server

E. HTTP method

Answer

API gateway is platform used to publish and manage APIs used for calling (proxy) various AWS backend services. In addition it adds functionality to internet-based mobile and enterprise applications. It is a managed service that provides automatic scaling for capacity, cost effective usage and integration with IAM. There is performance management enabled with throttling and caching to endpoints. API gateway endpoints are web servers, AWS services or Lambda functions. The API integrates an HTTP method (GET, PUT, POST) operation with an endpoint. There is no support for unencrypted endpoints considering they are external to the AWS cloud. (B,C,D)

Figure 11 API Gateway Architecture

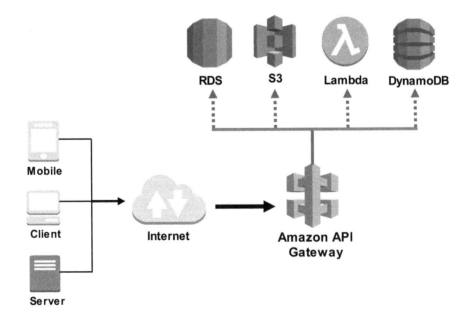

The tenant could for example create an API on the API gateway that invokes a Lambda function. The API call invokes (triggers) a Lambda function to execute some code. Lambda enables serverless architecture where the EC2 instances are dynamically provisioned. The tenant does not have to define any EC2 servers (instances). The Lambda function could for instance read, update or delete an item from a DynamoDB table or object from an S3 bucket.

The results are returned to the mobile application across the internet. API gateway more effectively leverages AWS services with ease while adding functionality for applications. The following example creates a serverless application based on RESTful API configured on the API gateway. It is used to update a DynamoDB table with a service request from a client.

1. Mobile client selects HTTPS endpoint (web page URL on S3 bucket) that calls RESTful API

2. RESTful API on API gateway invokes (triggers) Lambda function

3. Lambda functions execute code -> write data to database and/or return confirmation to mobile client

Question 24:

How is a volume selected (identified) when making an EBS Snapshot?

A. account id

B. volume id

C. tag

D. ARN

Answer

EBS volumes are identified by the assigned Amazon Resource Name (ARN) and used by *CreateSnapshot* (API) to create an EBS Snapshot. There is a unique ARN assigned to each AWS resource as a unique identifier to make requests, call services or specify IAM policies. (D)

Question 25:

What deployment service enables tenants to replicate an existing AWS stack?

A. Beanstalk

B. CloudFormation

C. RedShift

D. EMR

Answer

CloudFormation enables tenants to replicate an existing stack to a template (JSON script) with CloudFormer feature. That allows tenants for example to duplicate the same stack configuration to a different region. An AWS stack is comprised of all EC2 instances, AWS services and configuration associated with an application. That could include for example EC2 instances, ELB, Auto-Scaling, DynamoDB and Kinesis.

There is a significant amount of work required to replicate the same configuration through AWS management console. In addition you have to remember all settings and options that were enabled. CloudFormer can create a new template from existing infrastructure with customized settings such as bucket names and addressing that is unique. (B)

Question 26:

What three services can invoke a Lambda function?

A. SNS topic

B. CloudWatch event

C. EC2 instance

D. security group

E. S3 bucket notification

Answer

Lambda functions are invoked by AWS services and events associated with operational state of AWS infrastructure. it is AWS services such as S3, DynamoDB or API gateway that are used to invoke a Lambda function.

CloudWatch events and SNS are used extensively as well based on operational state changes that can trigger Lambda functions. Infrastructure components such as EC2 instances and security groups are not services. They are however monitored for state changes and traffic forwarded to logs. You can write Lambda functions to process Amazon Simple Notification Service notifications. When a message is published to an Amazon SNS topic, the service can invoke your Lambda function by passing the message payload as parameter. Your Lambda function code can then process the event. For example publish the message to other SNS topics or send it to other services. (A,B,E)

Question 27:

What two services enable automatic polling of a stream for new records only and forward them to an AWS storage service?

A. SNS

B. Kinesis

C. Lambda

D. DynamoDB

Answer

Kinesis data streams is used to capture and store big data (TB/hr) streams from hundreds of sources such as application logs, web transactions or location-tracking events for example. You can configure AWS Lambda to automatically poll your stream and process any new records. Lambda would polls the stream periodically for new records and forward them to a RedShift store for analysis. (B,C)

Question 28:

Your company is deploying a web site with dynamic content to customers in US, EU and APAC regions of the world. Content will include live streaming videos to customers. SSL certificates are required for security purposes. Select the AWS service delivers all requirements and provides the lowest latency?

A. DynamoDB

B. CloudFront

C. S3

D. Redis

Answer

AWS CloudFront is their Content Delivery Network (CDN) used to distribute web-based content to customers. It supports delivering dynamic web content that is cached to edge locations around the world. Caching web content locally to each region minimizes latency to customers and data transfer costs. There is support as well with CDN for deploying web endpoints with SSL certificates.

By contrast, S3 is only suitable for static web content and does not support SSL certificates. There is higher latency and costs for remote access from multiple regions. CloudFront stores content in an S3 bucket as an origin server however content is cached to edge locations. (B)

Question 29:

What are the advantages of Beanstalk? (Select two)

A. orchestration and deployment abstraction

B. template-oriented deployment service

C. easiest solution for developers to deploy cloud applications

D. does not support cloud containers

Answer

Beanstalk is a managed service that translates application developer code to Amazon AWS services. It isolates the developer from having to know deployment specifics and provide requirements through code. The requests could include anything from fault tolerant systems to data warehousing. (A,C)

Question 30:

You are a network analyst with JSON scripting experience and asked to select an AWS solution that enables automated deployment of cloud services. The template design would include a nondefault VPC with EC2 instances, ELB, Auto-Scaling and active/active failover. What AWS solution is recommended?

A. Beanstalk

B. OpsWorks

C. CloudTrail

D. CloudFormation

170

Answer

CloudFormation enables programmable infrastructure based on a JSON or YAML template that automates deployment of cloud services. The tenant creates a JSON template for instance for a fault tolerant database application. That requires EC2 instances for all servers associated with the application.
In addition storage is added and required services such as ELB, Auto-Scaling, CloudFront and DNS route 53. The failover RTO/RPO required would determine how the stacks are configured. The resulting design package is push button deployment that can be replicated to multiple regions. (D)

Question 31:

Select two statements that correctly describe OpsWorks?

A. Opsworks provides operational and configuration automation

B. OpsWorks is a lower cost alternative to BeanStalk

C. OpsWorks is primarily a monitoring service

D. Chef scripts (recipes) are a key aspect of OpsWorks

Answer

AWS OpsWorks is a service that automates configuration and operational management of AWS cloud environment. It supports Chef recipe scripts that automate cloud deployment tasks. It is often integrated with CloudFormation to provide operational, configuration and modeling services for cloud infrastructure. (A,D)

Question 32:

Your company has developed an IoT application that sends Telemetry data from 100,000 sensors. The sensors send a datapoint of 1 KB at one-minute intervals to a DynamoDB collector for monitoring purposes. What AWS stack would enable you to store data for real-time processing and analytics using BI tools?

A. Sensors -> Kinesis Data Streams -> Firehose -> DynamoDB -> RDS

B. Sensors -> Kinesis Data Streams -> Firehose -> DynamoDB -> S3

C. Sensors -> AWS IoT -> Firehose -> RedShift

D. Sensors -> Kinesis Data Streams -> Firehose -> RDS

Answer

Sensor datapoints are processed ingress to AWS cloud with AWS IoT or Kinesis data streams that can distribute the datapoint stream to a variety of AWS services. The purpose of RedShift is to provide a data warehouse solution where tenants can run sophisticated SQL queries and Business Intelligence reporting tools in real-time or offline. RedShift can analyze behaviors, patterns and trends for gaming, stocks, logs, twitter, sensor data and clickstreams. (C)

Question 33:

Your company has an application that was developed and migrated to AWS cloud. The application leverages some AWS services as part of the architecture. The stack includes EC2 instances, RDS database, S3 buckets, RedShift and Lambda functions. In addition there is IAM security permissions configured with defined users, groups and roles.

The application is monitored with CloudWatch and STS was recently added for permitting Web Identity Federation sign-on from Google accounts. You want a solution that can leverage the experience of your employees with AWS cloud infrastructure as well. What AWS service can create a template of the design and configuration for easier deployment of the application to multiple regions?

A. Snowball

B. Opsworks

C. CloudFormation

D. Beanstalk

Answer

CloudFormation enables tenants to develop templates based on YAML or JSON scripting for deploying stacks to AWS cloud. It is a service that is oriented to tenants that understand AWS infrastructure components. The AWS service makes deployment easier considering it leverages the script where configuration and components are specified. Tenants can then duplicate the stack to a different region, make modifications where applicable and maintain a template for similar deployments. (C)

Monitoring

Question 1:

What statement correctly describes CloudWatch operation within AWS cloud?

A. log data is stored indefinitely

B. log data is stored for 15 days

C. alarm history is never deleted

D. ELB is not supported

Answer

CloudWatch monitors data created by applications and systems messages that are sent to their log files. The log data is analyzed based on metrics and used to generate a CloudWatch log file. The results of alarms can be used to send email notifications or rules-based changes to AWS services. (A)

Question 2:

What are two AWS subscriber endpoint services that are supported with SNS?

A. RDS

B. Kinesis

C. SQS

D. Lambda

E. EBS

F. ECS

Answer

Simple Notification Service (SNS) supports SQS, Lambda, HTTP URL, email and SMS as subscriber endpoints for SNS. The tenant creates topics, adds subscribers to enable SNS notifications. Only standard SQS queues (no FIFO) are currently supported. (C,D)

Question 3:

What AWS services work in concert to integrate security monitoring and audit within a VPC? (Select three)

A. Syslog

B. CloudWatch

C. WAF

D. CloudTrail

E. VPC Flow Log

Answer

CloudWatch monitors and can send alerts when CloudTrail configured events such as security violations occur. For instance SNS notifications can be sent to tenant groups for a variety of CloudTrail events such as authentication attempts or security rule changes when IAM security policies are modified.

Figure 12 AWS Monitoring Architecture

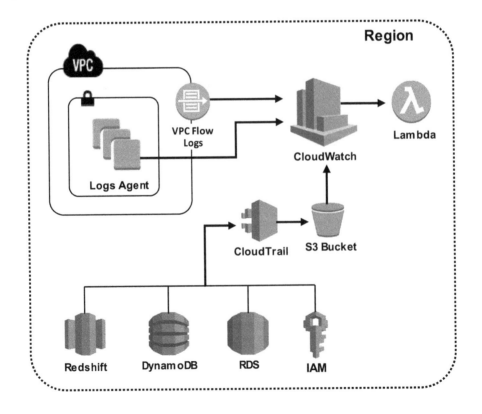

VPC Flow Logs monitor all ingress and egress IP traffic on network interfaces. Customized alarms are supported for specific events. That could include for instance when packets are denied or certain traffic types detected. CloudTrail log events and VPC Flow Logs are stored in Cloudwatch Log files for analysis and review. IAM user and IP address that made the network access attempts or policy changes can be identified from CloudWatch logs. (B,D,E)

Question 4:

How is CloudWatch integrated with Lambda functions? (Select two)

A. tenant must enable CloudWatch monitoring

B. network metrics such as latency are not monitored

C. Lambda functions are automatically monitored through Lambda service

D. log group is created for each event source

E. log group is created for each function

Answer

Lambda functions are automatically monitored through Lambda service and a log file is created for each function. There is real-time reporting of cloud metrics through CloudWatch that include total requests, latency, error rates and throttled requests. (C,E)

Question 5:

What two statements correctly describe AWS monitoring and audit operations?

A. CloudTrail captures API calls, stores them in an S3 bucket and generates a Cloudwatch event

B. CloudWatch alarm can send a message to a Lambda function

C. CloudWatch alarm can send a message to an SNS Topic that triggers an event for a Lambda function

D. CloudTrail captures all AWS events and stores them in a log file

E. VPC logs do not support events for security groups

Answer

CloudWatch is the AWS monitoring platform that is integrated with AWS services. It is used for monitoring operational status and performance metrics within the cloud. CloudWatch can send a message for instance to an SNS Topic that triggers an event for a Lambda function. CloudTrail is an audit service that generates logs for a variety of events and activities, stores them in an S3 bucket and generates a CloudWach event. The CloudWatch Events writes log files to an S3 bucket. Each log file contains one or more records. (A,C)

Question 6:

What is required for remote management access to your Linux-based instance?

A. ACL

B. Telnet

C. SSH

D. RDP

Answer

There is remote management access to EC2 instances for administrative purposes. The client software supported is SSH client with terminal emulation software such as PuTTY. Windows-based instances are accessed and managed with RDP. (C)

Question 7:

What are supported features of CloudWatch operation? (Select two)

A. CloudWatch does not support custom metrics

B. CloudWatch permissions are granted per feature and not AWS resource

C. collect and monitor operating system and application generated log files

D. AWS services automatically create logs for CloudWatch

E. CloudTrail generates logs automatically when AWS account is activated

Answer

Amazon CloudWatch is designed to collect and track metrics, monitor log files and set alarms for EC2 instances. CloudWatch user permissions are granted per feature and not per individual AWS resources. For example enabling read-only access to alarms, metrics and logs would apply to all AWS services for that user account. The CloudWatch policy is attached to the IAM user permissions. It is called identity-based policies instead of resource-based policies.

The tenant can configure and grant permissions to monitor various alarms, create events and monitor logs. CloudWatch architecture is based on monitoring application and operating system logs generated by EC2 instances. In addition there are some AWS services such as CloudTrail, Route 53 and VPC Flow Logs that create logs directly accessible to CloudWatch. The AWS service is granted sufficient permissions with an IAM role to publish logs to the specified log group in CloudWatch Logs. (B,C)

Question 8:

You are asked to select an AWS solution that will create a log entry anytime a snapshot of an RDS database instance and deletes the original instance. Select the AWS service that would provide that feature?

A. VPC Flow Logs

B. RDS Access Logs

C. CloudWatch

D. CloudTrail

Answer

There are a variety of monitoring features available for EC2 instances, AWS services (ELB, Route 53 etc) and database instances (DynamoDB, RDS etc). Each entity creates metrics, alarms and log files for analysis, troubleshooting and audit purposes. CloudTrail is a catch all monitoring service designed specifically to monitor, record and log all API calls to and between all entities.

It is used primarily to create an audit trail of all transactions made by all users, what they accessed and services primarily for security compliance purposes. For example CloudTrail would log the API call when a user creates a Snapshot of a security sensitive database or deletes an instance. In addition you can configure an SNS notification to notify you of the transaction. The log includes account username, API call and source IP address for audit purposes. (D)

Question 9:

What is required to enable application and operating system generated logs and publish to CloudWatch Logs?

A. Syslog

B. enable access logs

C. IAM cross-account enabled

D. CloudWatch Log Agent

Answer

EC2 instances for servers generate operating system and application generated log files. CloudWatch Logs Agent are enabled on each EC2 instance to create a log stream that publishes logs to CloudWatch Logs. (D)

Question 10:

What is the purpose of VPC Flow Logs?

A. capture VPC error messages

B. capture IP traffic on network interfaces

C. monitor network performance

D. monitor netflow data from subnets

E. enable Syslog services for VPC

Answer

The purpose of Flow Logs is to capture IP traffic on network interfaces for analysis and troubleshooting. Security rules for instance are listed in Flow Logs and any blocked traffic. The logs are stored and retrieved from Amazon CloudWatch service. (B)

Question 11:

Select two cloud infrastructure services and/or components included with default CloudWatch monitoring?

A. SQS queues

B. operating system metrics

C. hypervisor metrics

D. virtual appliances

E. application level metrics

Answer

By default, basic monitoring is enabled when you create a launch configuration using the AWS Management Console and detailed monitoring is enabled when you create a launch configuration using the AWS CLI or an API. Basic monitoring includes SQS queues and hypervisor performance metrics for EC2 intstances. Any application level or operating system level metrics are monitored by tenant software. (A,C)

Question 12:

What feature enables CloudWatch to manage capacity dynamically for EC2 instances?

A. replication lag

B. Auto-Scaling

C. Elastic Load Balancer

D. vertical scaling

Answer

CloudWatch alarms can be used to monitor CPU and memory thresholds for EC2 instances assigned to an Auto-Scaling group. Additional EC2 instances can be added to the Auto-Scaling group when performance thresholds are exceeded. There is a cooldown setting available with Auto-Scaling that specifies a minimum time before adding or releasing EC2 instances. The purpose is to stabilize operational state and prevent fluctuating performance from adding/terminating instances too fast during periods of changing workloads. (B)

Question 13:

What Amazon AWS service is deployed to monitor tenant remote access and various security errors including authentication retries?

A. SSH

B. Telnet

C. CloudFront

D. CloudWatch

Answer

CloudWatch is a versatile tool used extensively for monitoring performance and security access. Tenants access instances remotely across the internet through SSH encrypted connections started with PuTTY. Any errors including retry attempts and access denied is sent to a CloudWatch log. As with most Amazon AWS services, CloudWatch can be accessed from AWS management console, command line interface (CLI) and API. (D)

Question 14:

How does Amazon AWS isolate metrics from different applications for monitoring, store and reporting purposes?

A. EC2 instances

B. Beanstalk

C. CloudTrail

D. namespaces

E. Docker

Answer

Metrics for each application are assigned to a containers known as a namespace that isolate results for accurate reporting. (D)

Question 15:

What Amazon AWS service provides account transaction monitoring and security audit?

A. CloudFront

B. CloudTrail

C. CloudWatch

D. security group

Answer

The purpose of CloudTrail is to provide an audit trail of all transactions associated with an AWS account. It is used primarily for security compliance requirements and for optimizing security posture. The log files generated are integrated with CloudWatch for analysis and reporting.

It is important to know who is using your AWS account services for transactions such as sign-on, changing security settings and deleting volumes. Any audit trail is a key aspect of effective troubleshooting knowing when any recent change was made and who made it. Rules-based alerts are supported as well that are designed to alert staff when a transaction is not permitted or potentially affects network security. (B)

Question 16:

What two statements correctly describe CloudWatch monitoring of database instances?

A. metrics are sent automatically from DynamoDB and RDS to CloudWatch

B. alarms must be configured for DynamoDB and RDS within CloudWatch

C. metrics are not enabled automatically for DynamoDB and RDS

D. RDS does not support monitoring of operating system metrics

Answer

There are a standard group of supported metrics generated by DynamoDB and RDS database instances that are sent automatically to CloudWatch. By contrast, alarms are configured by the tenant within CloudWatch based on requirements and CloudWatch support. (A,B)

Question 17:

What AWS service can send notifications to customer smartphones and mobile applications with attached video and/or alerts?

A. EMR

B. Lambda

C. SQS

D. SNS

E. CloudTrail

Answer

SNS is integrated with CloudWatch and CloudTrail for sending alerts and publishing alerts to a variety of AWS services. For example there is S3 bucket event notification that is used to send an SNS notification when a new video file is stored to an S3 bucket. (D)

*** AWS Associate Practice Test ***

Test your knowledge with this sample test for AWS Certified Solutions Architect Associate exam. It is comprised of 60 selected questions and a time limit of 80 minutes. Each question is assigned one point and passing score is 72%.

- Read each question carefully and select the correct answer/s from the options provided. Use a pencil or erasable marker to select your answers.

- The answer key for the sample test is available after exam for you to verify your answers and tabulate results.

Question 1:

What are the minimum components required to enable a web-based application with public web servers and a private database tier? (Select three)

A. Internet gateway

B. Assign EIP addressing to database instances on private subnet

C. Virtual private gateway

D. Assign database instances to private subnet and private IP addressing

E. Assign EIP and private IP addressing to web servers on public subnet

Question 2:

What are supported features of CloudWatch operation? (Select two)

A. CloudWatch does not support custom metrics

B. CloudWatch permissions are granted per feature and not AWS resource

C. collect and monitor operating system and application generated log files

D. AWS services automatically create logs for CloudWatch

E. CloudTrail generates logs automatically when AWS account is activated

Question 3:

What Amazon AWS service is available for container management?

A. ECS

B. Docker

C. Kinesis

D. Lambda

Question 4:

What storage type is recommended for an online transaction processing (OLTP) application deployed to Multi-AZ RDS with significant workloads?

A. General Purpose SSD

B. Magnetic

C. EBS volumes

D. Provisioned IOPS

Question 5:

What class of EC2 instance type is recommended for database servers?

A. memory optimized

B. compute optimized

C. storage optimized

D. general purpose optimized

Question 6:

What three fault tolerant features are supported for S3 storage services?

A. cross-region replication

B. versioning must be disabled

C. cross-region asynchronous replication of objects

D. synchronous replication of objects within a region

E. multiple destination buckets

Question 7:

What is required to enable application and operating system generated logs and publish to CloudWatch Logs?

A. Syslog

B. enable access logs

C. IAM cross-account enabled

D. CloudWatch Log Agent

Question 8:

What are two advantages of cross-region replication of an S3 bucket?

A. cost

B. security compliance

C. scalability

D. Beanstalk support

E. minimize latency

Question 9:

What cloud compute (EC2 instances) components are configured by tenants and not Amazon AWS? (Select three)

A. hypervisor

B. upstream physical switch

C. virtual appliances

D. guest operating system

E. applications and databases

Question 10:

You have an Elastic Load Balancer assigned to a VPC with public and private subnets. ELB is configured to load balance traffic to a group of EC2 instances assigned to an Auto-Scaling group. What three statements are correct?

A. load balancer is assigned to a public subnet

B. network ACL is assigned to load balancer

C. security group is assigned to load balancer

D. cross-zone load balancing is not supported

E. load balancer forwards traffic to primary private IP address (eth0 interface) on each EC2 instance

Question 11:

What two features are supported with EBS volume Snapshot feature?

A. EBS replication across regions

B. EBS multi-zone replication

C. EBS single region only

D. full snapshot data only

E. unencrypted snapshot only

190

Question 12:

You have some developers working on code for an application and they require temporary access to AWS for up to an hour. What is the easiest AWS solution to provides access and minimize security exposure?

A. ACL

B. security group

C. IAM group

D. Security Token Service (STS)

E. EFS

Question 13:

What features distinguish Network ACLs from security groups? (Select three)

A. ACL filters at the subnet level

B. ACL is based on deny rules only

C. ACL is applied to instances and subnets

D. ACL is stateless

E. ACL supports a numbered list for filtering

Question 14:

What two statements correctly describe Auto-Scaling groups?

A. horizontal scaling of capacity

B. decrease number of instances only

C. EC2 instances are assigned to a group

D. database instances only

E. does not support Elastic Load Balancing

F. no support for multiple availability zones

Question 15:

You have been asked to setup a VPC endpoint connection between VPC and S3 buckets for storing backups and snapshots. What AWS component is currently required when configuring a VPC endpoint?

A. Internet gateway

B. NAT instance

C. Elastic IP

D. private IP address

E. Direct Connect

Question 16:

What are two primary advantages of DynamoDB?

A. SQL support

B. managed service

C. performance

D. CloudFront integration

Question 17:

What DNS attributes are configured when a default VPC is selected?

A. DNS resolution: yes
    DNS hostnames: yes

B. DNS resolution: yes
    DNS hostnames: no

C. DNS resolution: no
    DNS hostnames: yes

D. DNS resolution: no
    DNS hostnames: no

Question 18:

What are three primary characteristics of DynamoDB?

A. less scalable than RDS

B. static content

C. store metadata for S3 objects

D. auto-replication to three Availability Zones

E. high read/write throughput

Question 19:

What Amazon AWS service supports real-time processing of data stream from multiple consumers and replay of records?

A. DynamoDB

B. EMR

C. Kinesis data streams

D. SQS

E. RedShift

Question 20:

What are three primary reasons for deploying ElastiCache?

A. data security

B. managed service

C. Redis replication

D. durability

E. low latency

Question 21:

Select three requirements for configuring a Bastion host?

A. EIP

B. SSH inbound permission

C. default route

D. CloudWatch logs group

E. VPN

F. Auto-Scaling

Question 22:

What two features of an API Gateway minimize the effects of peak traffic events and minimize latency?

A. load balancing

B. firewalling

C. throttling

D. scaling

E. caching

Question 23:

What three characteristics differentiate Lambda from EC2 or containerization?

A. Lambda is based on Kinesis scripts

B. Lambda is serverless

C. tenant has ownership of EC2 instances

D. tenant has no control of EC2 instances

E. Lambda is a code-based service

F. Lambda supports only S3 and Glacier

Question 24:

What CIDR block range is supported for IPv4 addressing and subnetting within a single VPC?

A. /16 to /32

B. /16 to /24

C. /16 to /28

D. /16 to /20

Question 25:

What is the default behavior when adding a new subnet to a VPC? (Select two)

A. new subnet is associated with the main route table

B. new subnet is associated with the custom route table

C. new subnet is associated with any selected route table

D. new subnet is assigned to the default subnet

E. new subnet is assigned from the VPC CIDR block

Question 26:

You have enabled Amazon RDS database services in VPC1 for an application that has public web servers in VPC2. How do you connect the web servers to the RDS database instance so they can communicate considering the VPC's are in the same region?

A. VPC endpoints

B. VPN gateway

C. path-based routing

D. VPC peering

E. AWS Network Load Balancer

Question 27:

What are three methods of accessing DynamoDB for customization purposes?

A. CLI

B. AWS console

C. API programmatic call

D. vCenter

E. Beanstalk

Question 28:

What two attributes distinguish each pricing model?

A. reliability

B. amazon service

C. discount

D. performance

E. redundancy

Question 29:

What are two primary differences between Glacier and S3 storage services?

A. Glacier is lower cost

B. S3 is lower cost

C. Glacier is preferred for frequent data access with lower latency

D. S3 is preferred for frequent data access with lower latency

E. S3 supports larger file size

Question 30:

What are three primary **differences** between S3 vs EBS?

A. S3 is a multi-purpose public internet-based storage

B. EBS is directly assigned to a tenant VPC EC2 instance

C. EBS and S3 provide persistent storage

D. EBS snapshots are typically stored on S3 buckets

E. EBS and S3 use buckets to manage files

F. EBS and S3 are based on block level storage

Question 31:

What two statements correctly describe how to add or modify IAM roles to a running EC2 instance?

A. attach an IAM role to an existing EC2 instance from the EC2 console

B. replace an IAM role attached to an existing EC2 instance from the EC2 console

C. attach an IAM role to the user account and relaunch the EC2 instance

D. add the EC2 instance to a group where the role is a member

Question 32:

When is Direct Connect a preferred solution over VPN IPsec?

A. fast and reliable connection

B. redundancy is a key requirement

C. fast and easy to deploy

D. layer 3 connectivity

E. layer 2 connectivity

Question 33:

What two features correctly describe an Application Load Balancer (ALB)?

A. dynamic port mapping

B. SSL listener

C. layer 7 load balancer

D. backend server authentication

E. multi-region forwarding

Question 34:

What AWS storage solution allows thousands of EC2 instances to simultaneously upload, access, delete and share files?

A. EBS

B. S3

C. Glacier

D. EFS

E. Storage Gateway

Question 35:

Select two custom origin servers from the following?

A. S3 bucket

B. S3 object

C. EC2 instance

D. elastic load balancer

E. API gateway

Question 36:

How do you launch an EC2 instance after it is terminated? (Select two)

A. launch a new instance using the same AMI

B. reboot instance from CLI

C. launch a new instance from a Snapshot

D. reboot instance from management console

E. contact AWS support to reset

Question 37:

You recently made some configuration changes to an EC2 instance. You then launched a new EC2 instance from the same AMI however none of the settings were saved. What is the cause of this error?

A. did not save configuration changes to EC2 instance

B. did not save configuration changes to AMI

C. did not create new AMI

D. did not reboot EC2 instance to enable changes

Question 38:

What are two primary difference between Amazon S3 Standard and S3/RRS storage classes?

A. Amazon Standard does not replicate at all

B. RRS provides higher durability

C. RRS provides higher availability

D. RRS does not replicate objects as many times

E. application usage is different

Question 39:

What is required to Ping from a source instance to a destination instance?

A. Network ACL: not required
   Security Group: allow ICMP outbound on source/destination EC2 instances

B. Network ACL: allow ICMP inbound/outbound on source/destination subnets
   Security Group: not required

C. Network ACL: allow ICMP inbound/outbound on source/destination subnets
   Security Group: allow ICMP outbound on source EC2 instance
   Security Group: allow ICMP inbound on destination EC2 instance

D. Network ACL: allow TCP inbound/outbound on source/destination subnets
   Security Group: allow TCP and ICMP inbound on source EC2 instance

Question 40:

What is the recommended method for migrating (copying) an EC2 instance to a different region?

A. terminate instance, select region, copy instance to destination region

B. select AMI associated with EC2 instance and use *Copy AMI* option

C. stop instance and copy AMI to destination region

D. cross-region copy is not currently supported

Question 41:

What service can automate EBS snapshots (backups) for restoring EBS volumes?

A. CloudWatch event

B. SNS topic

C. CloudTrail

D. Amazon Inspector

E. CloudWatch alarm

Question 42:

What is required to copy an encrypted EBS snapshot cross-account? (Select two)

A. copy the unencrypted EBS snapshot to an S3 bucket

B. distribute the custom key from CloudFront

C. share the custom key for the snapshot with the target account

D. share the encrypted EBS snapshot with the target account

E. share the encrypted EBS snapshots publicly

F. enable root access security on both accounts

Question 43:

How are snapshots for an EBS volume created when it is the root device for an instance?

A. pause instance, unmount volume and snapshot

B. terminate instance and snapshot

C. unencrypt volume and snapshot dynamically

D. stop instance, unmount volume and snapshot

Question 44:

How are packets forwarded between public and private subnets within a VPC?

A. EIP

B. NAT

C. main route table

D. VPN

Question 45:

What statements correctly describe security groups within a VPC? (Select three)

A. default security group only permit inbound traffic

B. security groups are stateful firewalls

C. only allow rules are supported

D. allow and deny rules are supported

E. security groups are associated to network interfaces

Question 46:

How is routing enabled by default within a VPC for an EC2 instance?

A. add a default route

B. main route table

C. custom route table

D. must be configured explicitly

Question 47:

What is typically associated with Microservices? (Select two)

A. ALB

B. Kinesis

C. RDS

D. DynamoDB

E. ECS

F. EFS

Question 48:

What is the advantage of read-after-write consistency for S3 buckets?

A. no stale reads for PUT of any new object in all regions

B. higher throughput for all requests

C. stale reads for PUT requests in some regions

D. no stale reads for GET requests in a single regions

Question 49:

What two statements correctly describe versioning for protecting data at rest on S3 buckets?

A. enabled by default

B. creates snapshots

C. overwrites most current file version

D. restores deleted files

E. saves multiple versions of a single file

F. disabled by default

Question 50:

What attributes are selectable when creating an EBS volume for an EC2 instance? (Select three)

A. volume type

B. IOPS

C. region

D. CMK

E. EIP

Question 51:

How does AWS uniquely identify S3 objects?

A. bucket name

B. version

C. key

D. object tag

Question 52:

You have been asked to migrate a 10 GB unencrypted EBS volume to an encrypted volume for security purposes. What are three key steps required as part of the migration?

A. pause the unencrypted instance

B. create a new encrypted volume of the same size and availability zone

C. create a new encrypted volume of the same size in any availability zone

D. start converter instance

E. shutdown and detach the unencrypted instance

Question 53:

How is an EBS root volume created when launching an EC2 instance from a new EBS-backed AMI?

A. S3 template

B. original AMI

C. Snapshot

D. instance store

Question 54:

What is an EBS Snapshot? (select the best answer)

A. backup of an EBS root volume and instance data

B. backup of an EC2 instance

C. backup of configuration settings

D. backup of instance store

Question 55:

What feature is supported when attaching or detaching an EBS volume from an EC2 instance?

A. any available EBS volume can be attached and detached to an EC2 instance in the same region

B. any available EBS volume can be attached and detached to an EC2 instance that is cross-region

C. any available EBS volume can only be copied and attached to an EC2 instance that is cross-region

D. any available EBS volume can only be attached and detached to an EC2 instance in the same Availability Zone

Question 56:

How is a volume selected (identified) when making an EBS Snapshot?

A. account id

B. volume id

C. tag

D. ARN

Question 57:

What is a requirement for attaching VPC EC2 instances to on-premises clients?

A. Amazon Virtual private gateway (VPN)

B. Amazon Internet Gateway

C. VPN Connection

D. Elastic Load Balancer (ELB)

E. NAT

Question 58:

What three features are characteristic of Classic Load Balancers?

A. dynamic port mapping

B. path-based routing

C. SSL listener

D. backend server authentication

E. ECS

F. Layer 4 based load balancer

Question 59:

What consistency model is the default used by DynamoDB?

A. strongly consistent

B. eventually consistent

C. no default model

D. casual consistency

E. sequential consistency

Question 60:

What encryption support is available for tenants that are deploying AWS DynamoDB?

A. server-side encryption

B. client-side encryption

C. client-side and server-side encryption

D. encryption not supported

E. block level encryption

Answer Key

1. A,D,E
2. B,C
3. A
4. D
5. A
6. A,C,D
7. D
8. B,E
9. C,D,E
10. A,C,E
11. A,B
12. D
13. A,D,E
14. A,C
15. D
16. B,C
17. A
18. C,D,E
19. C
20. B,C,E
21. A,B,D
22. C,E
23. B,D,E
24. C
25. A,E
26. D
27. A,B,C
28. A,C
29. A,D
30. A,B,D

31. A,B
32. A
33. A,C
34. D
35. C,D
36. A,C
37. C
38. D,E
39. C
40. B
41. A
42. C,D
43. D
44. B
45. B,C,E
46. B
47. A,E
48. A
49. D,F
50. A,B,D
51. C
52. B,D,E
53. C
54. A
55. D
56. D
57. B
58. C,D,F
59. B
60. B

Supplemental Questions

1. What are three parts of an S3 object?

A. bucket name

B. key

C. endpoint

D. metadata

E. version id

Answer (B,D,E)

2. What are three examples of metadata attributes?

A. content-type

B. last-modified

C. cipher

D. content-length

E. bucket name

Answer (A,B,D)

3. What is true of S3 versioning?

A. permits multiple versions of an object

B. enabled by default

C. permits single version of an object

D. permits multiple versions of a bucket

Answer (A)

4. How are S3 objects restored from Glacier? (Select two)

A. restore a temporary copy to S3 bucket
B. there is no charge for service
C. initiate from Amazon S3 console only
D. initiate from AWS management console only
E. restore service is immediate

Answer (A,C)

5. What is the difference between Glacier standard and provisioned retrieval? (Select two)

A. standard retrieval is 3-5 hours
B. provisioned retrieval is 24 hours
C. standard retrieval is 1 hour
D. provisioned retrieval is immediate
E. standard retrieval is free

Answer (A,D)

6. What two statements correctly describe Pre-Signed URLs for S3 objects?

A. allows upload and download of S3 objects
B. IAM credentials are not required
C. IAM role credentials are required
D. allows download of public S3 objects only

Answer (A,B)

7. What are three limits for S3 buckets

A. 100 buckets per AWS account

B. nested buckets are permitted

C. bucket ownership is not transferable

D. 1000 objects per bucket

E. bucket names can start and end with periods

F. performance decreases as number of buckets increase

Answer (A,C,D)

8. What are three differences between Website and REST API endpoints when configuring an S3 bucket for web hosting?

A. REST API supports public and private content

B. REST API supports SSL

C. REST API support XML format response for error message handling

D. Website supports public and private content

E. Website supports SSL

F. Website support XML format response for error message handling

Answer (A,B,C)

9. What two statements correctly describe S3 pricing model?

A. data transfer to cloud is free

B. data transfer cross-region is free

C. PUT requests are free

D. data transfer from cloud is billed per GB/month

E. GET requests are billed per GB/month

Answer (A,D)

10. What statement is true of AMI contents?

A. template for EC2 instance only

B. contains application software and data

C. 10 GB minimum size

D. does not support Windows software

E. only a single EC2 instance can be launched

Answer (A)

11. What is block device mapping?

A. configuration for attaching data volumes/s to EC2 instance

B. configuration for attaching root device volume to EC2 instance

C. configuration for attaching EBS volumes only to EC2 instance

D. configuration for attaching data volumes/s to a database instance only

Answer (A)

12. What are launch permission for an AMI? (select three)

A. public

B. implicit

C. private

D. global

E. explicit

F. user

Answer (A,C,E)

13. What does *CreateImage API* accomplish? (Select two)

A. create S3-backed AMI
B. create EBS-backed AMI
C. reboots AMI
D. registers AMI
E. snapshots AMI

Answer (B,D)

14. What is the default launch behavior for a Linux AMI based EC2 instance? (Select three)

A. password authentication is disabled
B. key pairs are required
C. root login is disabled
D. root login is enabled
E. key pairs are disabled

Answer (A,B,C)

15. What is the default user account (username) that is permitted login to EC2 instance for Linux?

A. ec2-user
B. root
C. none
D. account id

Answer (A)

16. What AMI virtualization type provides best performance?

A. PV

B. HVM

C. ENI

D. C3

E. M3

Answer (B)

17. What are the correct use cases for each EBS volume type? (Select three)

A. General Purpose SSD (gp2) and smaller databases

B. Throughput Optimized HDD (magnetic st1) and EMR

C. Provisioned IOPS SSD (io1) and smaller databases

D. Provisioned IOPS SSD (io1) and RDS

E. General Purpose SSD (gp2) and larger databases

Answer (A,B,D)

18. Select three common causes that could prevent EC2 instances from launching?

A. security group and/or Network ACL are blocking traffic

B. public key file name and key pair name do not match

C. incorrect instance type is attached

D. private key file name and key pair name do not match

E. AWS account limits are exceeded

Answer (A,D,E)

19. What are three key features of SQS?

A. creates centralized applications

B. push-based

C. priority queues supported

D. poll-based

E. creates loosely coupled distributed applications

F. RDS used for message store

Answer (C,D,E)

20. Select three AWS services that use resource-based policies?

A. S3

B. Glacier

C. Lambda

D. RDS

E. DynamoDB

Answer (A,B,C)

21. How are identity-based IAM policies used with AWS? (Select two)

A. identity-based policies are attached to user, group or role

B. EC2, RDS and DynamoDB use identity-based policies

C. identity-based policies are attached to user only

D. identity-based policies require a trust policy as well

E. EC2, RDS and DynamoDB use resource-based policies

Answer (A,B)

22. What statement correctly describe VPC peering architecture?

A. multiple virtual VPC peering connections are permitted between two VPC's

B. traffic is encrypted across peering links

C. only a single VPC peering connection is permitted between two VPC's

D. internet gateways are required

Answer (C)

23. What two statements describe RDS architecture?

A. SSH root access to database instances is not available to tenants

B. database instance can contain multiple user created tables

C. maximum of 10 database instances

D. read replicas are not enabled for standard storage class

Answer (A,B)

24. How does an EC2 instance and RDS instance share the same security group?

A. DB security group

B. VPC security group

C. EC2 security group

D. NACL subnet group

Answer (B)

25. What is the default setting for RDS security?

A. network access is turned off to an RDS database instance by default

B. network access is permitted for an RDS database instance by default

C. all outbound traffic is permitted by default

D. all inbound traffic is permitted by default

Answer (A)

26. What three metrics are used for RDS billing?

A. instance class

B. hourly access

C. storage usage (GB/month)

D. subscription

E. demand

Answer (A,B,C)

27. What AWS service can be used to trigger a notification message to social media network based on a DynamoDB attribute update?

A. Lambda

B. RDS

C. CloudTrail

D. CloudWatch

E. VPC Log

Answer (A)

28. What SQS feature enables multiple readers (applications) to access the same queue so messages are not processed multiple times?

A. queue timer

B. message locking

C. TTL timer

D. visibility timeout

Answer (D)

29. What IAM security class enables temporary access for a user, application or service?

A. IAM dynamic

B. IAM STS

C. IAM group

D. IAM user

E. IAM role

Answer (E)

30. How do you create a CloudWatch events rule that triggers on an event?

A. select event source, add target and attach IAM role

B. select event rule, attach IAM user and add target

C. select event, add custom metric and add trigger

D. select trigger, add rule and attach IAM role

Answer (A)

31. What is required to enable Route 53 Latency-based routing (LBR)? (Select two)

A. assign IP address to all ELB

B. assign AWS endpoints as LBR-enabled

C. create DNS record set

D. mark record set as LBR-enabled

E. configure Alias records for all ELB endpoints

Answer (C,D)

32. What is the AWS endpoint configured for clients that are accessing an EC2 instance across the internet?

A. IP address of Route 53 name server

B. IP address of Elastic Load Balancer

C. DNS name of Elastic Load Balancer

D. IP address of web server

Answer (C)

33. What three statements accurately describe the differences between Kinesis streams and Kinesis Firehose?

A. Kinesis Firehose is an analytical tool

B. Kinesis data streams capture, process and analyze streams

C. Kinesis Firehose captures and loads Kinesis data stream to data store

D. Kinesis data streams is a fully managed service

E. Kinesis data streams forwards traffic to consumers first

Answer (B,C,E)

34. How is scale in and scale out capacity triggered for an Auto-Scaling group?

A. warmup timer

B. cooldown timer

C. threshold attribute

D. CloudWatch alarm

E. CloudTrail

F. SNS

Answer (D)

35. How is a user or application identity verified when accessing AWS programmatically with API calls?

A. IAM role

B. AWS account id

C. access keys

D. public key

E. root user password

F. STS credentials

Answer (C)

36. What three AWS services enable Multi-AZ redundancy as a default (native) feature?

A. EC2 instance

B. RDS

C. S3

D. Auto-Scaling

E. SQS

Answer (B,C,E)

37. What is the default health check for an Elastic Load Balancer of an EC2 instance?

A. open a TCP connection to instance

B. ping instance IP address

C. disabled

D. open HTTPS connection to instance

Answer (A)

38. What is the default TTL for a DNS Route 53 record?

A. 60 seconds

B. based on record type

C. 10 seconds

D. no default value

Answer (D)

39. What are the advantages of using Web Identity Federation with well-known identity providers (i.e Facebook, Google) for mobile web-based applications? (Select two)

A. do not have to create custom sign-in for customers

B. AWS supports multiple OpenID Connect (OIDC) providers

C. lower latency

D. IAM role is not required

E. SAML provided the session token

Answer (A,B)

40. You have developed a mobile application on AWS cloud that must be accessible from any wireless hotspot in the USA. In addition the web-based application should only be publicly accessible to registered users. What AWS connectivity option is the most cost effective?

A. VPN IPsec

B. Direct Connect

C. SSL

D. DMVPN

E. BGP

Answer (C)

41. What three features are only supported by an application load balancer?

A. WAF
B. ECS dynamic port mapping
C. IPv6
D. SSL termination
E. cross-zone load balancing

Answer (A,B,C)

42. What AWS load balancer type is required to inspect HTTPS headers for content-based routing?

A. classic load balancer
B. application load balancer
C. network load balancer
D. Route 53 load balancer

Answer (B)

43. What statement correctly describes VPC Flow Log operation?

A. flow logs do not capture real-time log streams for network interfaces
B. flow logs capture real-time log streams for EC2 instance network interfaces
C. flow logs can't be created for network interfaces of AWS services (ELB etc)
D. flow logs do not capture traffic from security groups

Answer (A)

44. You are troubleshooting network connectivity to an Amazon AWS application in a private subnet and have verified access to public subnet instances. Select two components you should you verify as part of your troubleshooting process?

A. NAT instance is enabled

B. main route table is correct

C. custom route table is correct

D. EIP is assigned to instances in private subnet

Answer (A,B)

45. What AWS services are available to encrypt data at rest on S3? (Select two)

A. S3 server-side encryption with customer-provided keys

B. SSL certificate

C. S3 server-side encryption with AWS Key Management Service (KMS)

D. S3 bucket policies

E. IAM instance profile

Answer (A,C)

46. What happens to an EC2 instance that fails a health check? (Select two)

A. ELB removes the instance from the Auto-Scaling group

B. ELB stops the instance and Auto-Scaling group removes instance

C. Auto-Scaling group removes the instance

D. ELB reboots instance and performs EC2 health check to verify state

E. ELB no longer forwards traffic to that instance

Answer (C,E)

47. Your company is deploying an application in a single VPC with EC2 instances for web servers and a backend RDS database instance. The web servers will be deployed to a public subnet and RDS to a private subnet. Customers will access the application from a standard web browser across the internet. What is required to deploy the application with in-transit encryption and WAF? (Select two)

A. classic load balancer

B. application load balancer

C. SSL certificate

D. CloudFront

Answer (B,C)

48. What occurs when a tenant does not configure an RDS backup window when creating a database instance? (Select two)

A. automated backups are disabled by default

B. AWS assigns a default 30-minute backup window at random

C. default backup window is selected from an 8-hour block of time per region

D. database instance wont launch

Answer (B,C)

49. What occurs when the backup retention period is not configured by tenant for RDS? (Select two)

A. RDS defaults the retention period to one day if configured using RDS API or the AWS CLI

B. Backup retention period can be configured for unlimited backup retention

C. Backup retention period can be configured for a maximum of 30 days

D. RDS defaults retention period to 7 days if configured from AWS console

Answer (A,D)

50. What features are supported with Redis and not with Memcached caching engine? (Select three)

A. Multi-AZ replication (asynchronous)
B. complex data objects (hash, list, sets)
C. vertical and horizontal scaling
D. database persistence store
E. unlimited value size per key

Answer (A,B,D)

51. What are two reasons for deploying ElastiCache?

A. faster database queries with lower latency
B. offload management, monitoring, and operation of in-memory cache environment
C. optimize security across the internet
D. store dynamic content for web-based applications
E. replaces some database services for SQL applications

Answer (A,B)

52. Select three features of API gateway architecture?

A. API gateway does not run within an Amazon AWS VPC
B. API Gateway endpoints are public
C. API gateway is a proxy to backend AWS services
D. API gateway is not a managed service
E. API gateway is assigned to a single VPC
F. API gateway supports cross-region forwarding

Answer (A,B,C)

53. What are three advantages of API gateway services?

A. automatic DDoS protection (SYN floods)

B. caching API calls to prevent redundant calls to backend services

C. leverage existing IAM and Cognito configuration to authorize access to APIs

D. all endpoints are unencrypted

E. database services are eliminated

Answer (A,B,C)

54. What is the architecture used by API gateway?

A. API gateway is an intermediary for developing web-based content

B. API gateway is a proxy server for database services

C. APIs connect client software to AWS services for creating applications

D. APIs are configured on client software that connect to VPC instances only

E. API gateway is a firewall for internet-based applications

Answer (C)

55. What does API gateway do with requests when caching is not enabled and throttling limits are reached?

A. all requests pass through to the backend service until the account level throttling limits are reached

B. API Gateway will shed necessary amount of requests and send only the defined limit to the back-end

C. API Gateway will return a cached response for duplicate requests for a customizable time

D. packets are dropped and session ended with error message returned

Answer (A)

56. What database service supports document and key-value store models?

A. RDS

B. PostgreSQL

C. Aurora

D. DynamoDB

Answer (D)

57. What two statements correctly describe ElastiCache characteristics?

A. ElastiCache latency is lower than native database access

B. ElastiCache is not as durable

C. ElastiCache is extremely durable

D. Caching increases latency and durability

E. ElastiCache latency is higher than native database access

Answer (A,B)

58. What are two use cases for Amazon Simple Workflow Service (SWF)?

A. verify each step for a structured application workflow

B. provides queuing of messages for distributed applications

C. verify multi-step processes are completed within a time interval

D. provides temporary sequencing of application processes

Answer (A,C)

59. Select two primary advantages of Aurora for RDS SQL databases?

A. less replication lag

B. lower recovery time

C. fully managed

D. supports complex queries and analysis

Answer (A,B)

60. What two statements characterize DynamoDB usage?

A. designed for basic store and lookup of information

B. designed for complex table queries and analysis

C. replicates tables to three Availability Zones

D. does not support cross-region replication

E. cannot store metadata for S3 objects

F. cannot store user state attributes

Answer (A,C)

61. What statements correctly describe Amazon AWS Key Management Service? (Select three)

A. managed encryption service

B. centralized access control and audit of master keys for encrypting and decrypting user data

C. native integration with S3 and EBS

D. does not support CloudTrail

E. distributed access model

Answer (A,B,C)

62. What is the primary difference between the models for customer-managed managed (KMI) encryption keys?

A. key storage

B. key management

C. encryption method

D. key rotation

Answer (A)

63. What are two primary characteristics of EC2 placement groups that enable higher performance? (Select two)

A. placement groups do not span Availability Zones
B. proximity of cluster instances enable higher throughput
C. enhanced networking instance type not supported
D. multiple unique instance types per group recommended
E. placement groups cannot span peering VPCs

Answer (A,B)

64. What are three advantages of migrating web content to CloudFront?

A. CDN ready global infrastructure with elastic capacity
B. CloudFront maintains copies of objects in multiple edge locations globally
C. CloudFront keeps persistent connections with origin servers to lower latency
D. CloudFront caches all content in DynamoDB for faster distribution
E. CloudFront supports ElastiCache as an origin server
F. CloudFront encrypts data in-transit to improve throughput

Answer (A,B,C)

65. What occurs when ELB connection draining is enabled? (Select two)

A. ELB waits for in-flight requests to complete before EC2 instance deregistered
B. EC2 instances remain running after being deregistered from an ELB
C. EC2 instances assigned to Auto-Scaling group are terminated after in-flight requests completed
D. ELB waits for in-flight requests to complete before terminating all EC2 instances

Answer (A,B)

66. When must EC2 instances be registered manually to ELB?

A. EC2 instances that were added during a suspension period

B. EC2 instances have enhanced networking enabled

C. EC2 instances that were added to a placement group

D. EC2 instances span an Availability Zone

Answer (A)

67. What AWS services or instance permit full administrative privilege for tenant access? (Select three)

A. Beanstalk

B. EC2

C. RDS

D. ElastiCache

E. EMR

F. Aurora

Answer (A,B,E)

68. What three monitoring services are free from AWS?

A. basic monitoring metrics for Amazon EC2 instances in 5 minute intervals

B. all metrics for EBS, ELB and RDS DB instances

C. detailed monitoring with 10 metrics for CloudWatch Logs

D. basic monitoring metrics for Amazon EC2 instances in 1 minute intervals

E. 10 million API request per month

F. 10 high resolution alarms

Answer (A,B,C)

69. You have decided to select HVM for support of enhanced networking. What current generation EC2 instance type requires HVM and do not support PV virtualization type?

A. T2,M4

B. M3

C. C4,R4

D. C3

E. T1,M1,C1

Answer (A,C)

70. What are two advantages of consolidated billing?

A. tracking multiple cost centers

B. volume pricing discounts

C. additional free usage tiers

D. billing statements are encrypted

Answer (A,B)

Study Tools

The following are links to some additional study tools. The AWS labs provide practical experience with a variety of topics such as creating EC2 instances, S3 buckets, IAM security and VPC configuration.

https://aws.amazon.com/getting-started/labs/

Amazon Books

- AWS Certified Solutions Architect Associate Exam Study Notes
- Cloud Computing: Architecture Fundamentals for Cloud Systems

Udemy Practice Tests

https://www.udemy.com/aws-certified-solutions-architect-associate-exam-extended/

Lightning Source UK Ltd.
Milton Keynes UK
UKHW051804240419
341548UK00010B/175/P